Examining Oral English in Schools

'No hearing without judging'

—H. H. PRICE

Examining
Oral English
in Schools

P. J. HITCHMAN M.Ed., Ph.D.

Lecturer in Speech, Department of Education, University of Nottingham

METHUEN & CO LTD · LONDON

First published 1966
by Methuen & Co Ltd, 11 New Fetter Lane London EC4
© P. J. Hitchman 1966
Printed in Great Britain
by Cox & Wyman Ltd, London, Fakenham and Reading

Contents

Preface

A new, and what promises to be a continuing, interest in the examination of oral English is now being shown in schools, colleges and various examining bodies throughout the country. This book is intended to help teachers to understand the problems involved in the testing of spoken English and to show how, with a minimum of expert help, they can design their own tests, conduct them and evaluate the results.

The first part of this book attempts (1) to assess the needs of the community in terms of the spoken English ability of its members (that is to say, what kinds of ability in spoken English should be fostered for the benefit of the community), and also the needs of its members as individuals, (2) to suggest the sorts of speech activity in school that can best satisfy these needs.

The second, and larger, section deals with testing and the assessment of achievement. It explores the subjective nature of testing, examines the problems involved in the candidate–assessor relationship, attempts to show why judges tend to disagree and suggests means whereby this disagreement may be minimized, i.e. how tests may be made more reliable. It proposes model designs for tests and makes practical suggestions for their conduct. It focuses attention on the most important factor in testing, the *assessor*, and suggests a unit of training in assessment for interested teachers. Appendices contain test-material, a specimen Rating Scale and mark sheet, a glossary of speech terms and suggestions for further reading.

There are at present in use three methods of testing the spoken

English ability of schoolchildren. The first two are face-to-face tests in which both candidate and examiner(s) are present; the third is a combination of a face-to-face assessment and a tape-test assessment.

1. A 'private' test in which the only people present in the examination-room are candidate and examiner (usually only one). Tests conducted in this way are those of the Joint Matriculation Board and of the University of London School Examinations Council for their school candidates, and of the Institutes of Education of the Universities of Durham and Nottingham for their training-college students.

2. A 'public' test which is conducted by one examiner, the candidate being assessed by this examiner and several others in the room in the presence of a group of his or her peers (often classmates) and perhaps a few teachers and parents. The English Speaking Board conducts its tests for all its candidates in this way.

3. A 'private' test in which only examiner and candidate are present, the examiner making a tape-recording of the proceedings at the same time as he is conducting the examination and making his assessments. The recording is then available for moderation by a chief assessor and one or more additional assessors. The Brighton Education Authority has sponsored the experimental testing done in its schools in this way for several years. It is possible that a tape-test as an element in the technique of assessment of Oral English may eventually be used by some of the Regional Boards for the Certificate of Secondary Education.

This book deals only with tests of the first two types, the face-to-face tests. The writer has subjected the 'private' test (No. 1 above) to rigorous experimental examination covering those elements most commonly found in tests for schools – Prose Reading and Conversation, and those usually found in tests for training colleges – Prose Reading, Poetry Speaking, Speech Making, Conversation. His experimental results when combined with those from American research strongly suggest that a test offering these elements will, under certain safeguards, be as valid and reliable as tests in written English. No research results have yet been presented for the 'public' test (No. 2 above). However, the test being similar in some respect to the 'private' test, the writer has extended the assumption of validity and reliability to the 'public' face-to-face test (while being well aware of the need to submit this type of test to rigorous investigation), and thus has felt able to cover both these types of test in this book.

The tape-test as used by the Brighton Authority is really an extension of test (No. 1 above), since the tapes are simply used for purposes of moderation, i.e. of standardization of the face-to-face results. However, there are important differences between the Nos. 1 and 2 type and the No. 3 type tests. First, in the Nos. 1 and 2 the candidate reads from a distance of 15 to 18 feet to the examiner (i.e. he has to project his communication by the proper use of voice and articulation), while in the No. 3 test there is no arrangement yet for this projection from a distance, and he reads into a microphone at close range. (This is not to say that reading at close range may not be just as satisfactory a physical condition of testing the reading aloud of prose as reading at 15 or 18 feet; it is certainly a *different* physical condition requiring a different use of voice and the articulatory processes. Since the voice is a vital bearer of meaning and feeling this is indeed a very considerable difference.) Second, the presence and operation by the assessor of a recording machine introduce a new physical factor into the total examination situation and a new psychological one, since the candidate will know that, in spite of anonymity, he is on record. The writer considers it important that testing by tapes alone should not be used until such time as the validity and reliability of such testing have been experimentally demonstrated. We cannot transfer our recognition of the validity and reliability of the face-to-face test to the tape-test because of a vital perceptual difference: tape-listening cuts out all the visual cues which form a part of the aura of meaning and feeling generated in the examiner/examinee situation (and so may cause the tape-listener to lose some of the aural cues as well); hence the examiner/examinee situation is a totally different one. (An observer is not in the same speaker–listener relationship as a participant–observer, and therefore is not in the same assessing situation, and an observer deprived of all but the aural cues is in a relationship still further removed – in fact, in no speaker–listener relationship at all. This is not to say that the tape-judge is incapable of making a valid judgement, but simply to show that judgements will be based on a very different assessing situation from that involved in face-to-face assessment.)

Because nothing is as yet known of its validity and reliability tape-testing has not been discussed in this book.

The writer wishes to thank the Brighton Education Authority for its courtesy in allowing him to observe its 1964 tests in progress and to discuss the testing procedures with those operating them. He also wishes to thank the same Authority and the authorities of the Herbert Strutt School, Belper, for making available to him copies of the reading material for their Spoken English tests used in recent years (printed in Appendix 1). Some of that supplied by the Herbert Strutt School has been the subject of the writer's adjudications of the school's annual Spoken English Competition. Thanks are also due to the Joint Matriculation Board for permission to use the linked passages Nos. 1–3 (inclusive) and the single passages Nos. 19, 21, 22.

The writer is deeply grateful to Professor Samuel Becker, Head of the Department of Speech of the University of Iowa, for reading and criticizing the manuscript and for making many useful suggestions.

Acknowledgements

Acknowledgement and thanks are due to the following for permission to quote in Appendix 1 from works in their copyright:

The Joint Matriculation Board for Extracts 1, 2 and 3; Leonard Woolf for Extract 2, from *Orlando* by Virginia Woolf; J. M. Dent & Sons and the Literary Executors of the Dylan Thomas Estate for Extract 3, from *Quite Early One Morning* by Dylan Thomas; the Director of Education, Brighton Local Education Authority for Extracts 4 and 5, *Leisure* and *Fashion*; Longmans Green for Extract 6, from *Ring of Bright Water* by Gavin Maxwell; Hodder and Stoughton for Extract 8, from *The Ascent of Everest* by Sir John Hunt; Chatto and Windus for Extract 10, from *The Spirit of St. Louis* by Colonel Charles Lindberg; Michael Joseph for Extract 11, from *The Kraken Wakes* by John Wyndham; A. D. Peters & Co. for Extract 12, from *Memoirs of a Sword Swallower* by Dan Mannix; Stevie Smith for Extract 13, from a broadcast; Michael Joseph for Extract 14, from *Village School* by 'Miss Read'; William Heinemann for Extract 15, from *The Forsyte Saga* by John Galsworthy; Odhams Books Ltd. for Extract 16, from *Painting as a Pastime* by Sir Winston Churchill; Faber & Faber for Extract 22, from *Clea* by Lawrence Durrell; John Betjeman for Extract 23, *How to Look at a Church*; Alex Comfort for Extract 24, from a broadcast; R. A. Weale for Extract 25, from a broadcast; Macmillan for Extract 25 (a), *The Discovery* by J. C. Squire.

The author and publisher would like to make general acknowledgement for those passages whose source they have been unable to trace.

PART I

The Background

CHAPTER I *Introduction*

The schools of Great Britain have been for so long without the formal testing of spoken English that it is worth while inquiring why there is a sudden national interest in this type of examination. It is probable that in a few years large numbers of secondary school boys and girls will be able to take a test at age 15 or 16 and receive, on passing, a certificate of attestation. It is true there are tests already in existence but these touch only a small proportion of the school population. Now, with the new London University 'O Level' test and the tests in spoken English that form a part of the examinations of the regional bodies promoting the new Certificate of Secondary Education, there is a widening of appeal to take in all kinds of secondary schools and vastly increased numbers of candidates. Why is there this urgent post-war demand?

The writer sees it as a belated recognition of the importance of spoken English in the world of today. The nation has already demanded of our schools the extension of the teaching of science and mathematics; it is beginning to demand an extension of the teaching of good speech. The fight for national survival in the world today requires not only massive and widespread scientific and technical 'know-how' (and an understanding of underlying basic principles) but also a widespread power of communication, the ability to talk plain English and to listen intelligently so that there shall be as full a measure of understanding as possible between speakers and listeners. Today the general public as a whole, and those engaged in education in particular, are more speech-conscious than ever before;

3

it is seen that speech permeates all our human activities, industrial, commercial, social. (It permeates the classroom.) Everybody uses the telephone, more and more people are achieving positions in life in which they need to persuade others, or to inform them or to control them tactfully, or to conduct some form of public relations, however humble – and all by means of spoken language. Everybody is in contact with the power of language by being made a listener to the radio or a viewer at the cinema or the television set. Modern methods of communication have brought to educationists a sharp new awareness of the potency of human speech and a determination to give some sort of training in spoken language in school and college.

The growing demand for the institution of tests at a popular level is, in fact, a growing demand for the teaching of good speech in schools.

In the past there has been an almost total neglect of the teaching of certain aspects of spoken English – the more important. The schools and training colleges of this country have a long and heroic tradition of teaching Reading (aloud) and Recitation,* but the systematic development of the powers of spoken language in pupil and student has not generally received attention. Written language is not acquired naturally; it has to be taught. Speech is naturally acquired and training has tended to be incidental – mainly by precept, example and practice (of course, not to be despised) in the home and the school. It is now realized that, while no subject can be taught properly without some incidental, and on occasion purposive, training in language-management appropriate to that subject – and therefore language training is the legitimate business of every teacher in every subject – improvement can be brought about by the direct and systematic teaching of spoken English. (Consider, in a

* In 1847, Reading, including the reading of Poetry, became a subject of examination, conducted by Her Majesty's Inspectors, in the Christmas Examinations (for training colleges) of the Education Department in Whitehall. To this was added in 1863 'Repetition from Memory'. Both remained as examination subjects for first- and second-year students throughout the nineteenth century.

4

comparable field, the enormous 'mushroom' growth of the teaching of English as a second language for foreigners in language schools and language laboratories.) Spoken English is in process of being upgraded to the status of a school subject; specialist teachers trained in schools of Speech and Drama and in training colleges are being appointed to the staffs of Local Education Authorities and of schools and colleges.* It is a short step to making this new 'subject' examinable.

Testing will tend (is, in fact, already tending) to raise the status of spoken English as a subject taught in schools, for a subject that is tested is inevitably considered more important than one that is not. The real value of the spoken English test lies not in the piece of paper the successful candidate receives (although this may be of growing value in the years to come) but in the effect its institution has on the teaching and learning of spoken English. It becomes a focus for the pupil's work, an end towards which to strive, a powerful motivating force, for nothing gives such an edge to practical training as practical examination. It compels organization of speech work, the careful thinking out of aims and method, regularity of practice and an appreciation of standards. The better a man speaks, the clearer he thinks. Good speech gives its possessor confidence and contributes to his grasp of the world around him; slovenly speech is symptomatic of an attitude to the organization of its possessor's experiences.

The test in spoken English has, or can have, another value, a very important one. If the test is suitably designed its results can pinpoint the strengths and weaknesses of the candidate's oral English. This is especially valuable to candidate and teacher if the former can undergo a series of tests at regular intervals throughout his secondary school career, or if there is at least one test some time before he leaves school; that is to say, if the timing of the test or tests allows an appropriate length of time for attention in school to weaknesses revealed.

What should be the form of a test in spoken English? What should be its content? What do we want to test? (If we can answer

* There is a bright future in education for competent specialist teachers of Speech and Drama.

this question we shall then have to ask: Can it be tested? How? By whom?)

Any worth-while test should surely bear some relation to the course of training given in school or college to which it is the sequel, and the training should spring from an assessment of the needs of the community and the individuals who compose it.

We must now therefore consider what these needs are and how they may be met.

CHAPTER 2   *Articulacy*

The needs of the nation and the individual

In the middle of last century the nation needed a literate population, one that could read and write. Its leaders took the drastic step of instituting compulsory education for all. A hundred years later the need is largely satisfied.*

Into this world, already literate, says Lewis,†[3] comes today a renaissance of the spoken word. We are all influenced by the modern speech-machines – the telephone, gramophone, wireless, talkie, television, tape-recorder. In ancient Greece and Rome the spoken word was all-powerful; the teaching of rhetoric was one of the important bases of education. Mark Antony is for us the symbol of the power of speech. Now once again, after centuries of the growing use of the written word, the leaders of men turn to the spoken word as a medium of mass-communication.

Today the need is for 'spoken literacy'. The Greeks and Romans saw the need for an articulate ruling-class and provided training in rhetoric; today we see the need for an articulate mass-population, and are girding ourselves to provide training in speech. We have

* Not completely. M. M. Lewis gives figures: totally illiterate (unable even to sign name), 2 in 1,000; crudely illiterate (can sign name, write simple words, read isolated words such as street names, interpret simple sentences), 10 in 1,000; functionally illiterate (unable to read a simple paragraph in a popular newspaper or write a simple letter), 36 in 1,000.[4]

† A number in this position refers to the appropriate numbered reference at the end of the chapter.

come tardily to realize that adequate verbal communication at all levels – in industry, business, government service – is vital to the well-being of the nation. Perhaps more slowly still it has been borne in upon us that it is vital also socially as well if class barriers are ever to be broken down. The Newsom Report says, 'This matter of communication affects all aspects of social and intellectual growth. There is a gulf between those who have and the many who have not sufficient command of words to be able to listen and discuss rationally; to express ideas and feelings clearly; and even to have any ideas at all. We simply do not know how many are frustrated in their lives by inability ever to express themselves adequately; or how many never develop intellectually because they lack the words with which to think and to reason. This is a matter as important to economic life as it is to personal living; industrial relations as well as marriage come to grief on failures in communication.'[6]

The promotion of articulacy has not always been the main aim. A hundred years ago excellence in reading and recitation was the prime aim in the teaching of spoken English. Reading aloud was a convenient means of teaching a child the contents of his geography or history primer, recitation an attractive form of elocution which would show whether he had learned his poem by heart. Teacher-trainees were taught to read and recite so that they could teach their children to read and recite. The primacy of reading and recitation continued throughout the nineteenth and well into the twentieth century.

For some time there has been a strong reaction against this view of speech-training; 'elocution' has become a term of contempt. Today, while the aesthetic and personal values of reading aloud and recitation ('oral interpretation' in America) are recognized, their practical value is searchingly questioned and their importance in the school curriculum is considerably diminished. The Norwood Report of 1943 pointed the way to a new speech-training with aims and values geared to the needs of the second half of the twentieth century. The Report complained that there was a serious failure in the secondary schools in training pupils to think clearly and to express themselves lucidly on paper and in speech; they were often at a loss in communicating what they wished to communicate in clear and simple sentences and in expressive and audible tone.[7] The McNair Report of 1944 summed up the language requirements of a teacher (they are also the requirements of his pupils): 'Three things are involved – clear and, if possible, pleasant speech; the power to say and write what one means; and the capacity to direct one's understanding to what other people say and write.' On the same page (86) the Report speaks of children's 'need for giving constructive and creative expression to what they experience, feel and think.'[5]

Bernstein has shown that nearly a third of Britain's population is likely to be 'spoken illiterates'. As a result of his experimental work with groups of middle and lower working-class adolescent boys he postulates two forms of spoken language in England – a 'restricted code' (or, as he has also called it, a 'public language') and an 'elaborated code[1] (or 'formal language'). These codes he regards as a function of different social structures.

'Spoken illiterates' have access only to the former, a language of restricted speech structures, one unadapted for communication outside the group (the *how* of communication heavily burdened with implicit meanings available only to the group), unapt for abstractions, poor in adjectival and adverbial enrichments: features – short, grammatically simple, often unfinished sentences, active voice only; simple and repetitive use of conjunctions; little use of subordinate clauses; inability to hold a formal subject through a short sequence, etc. This 'code' tends to separate the social classes, to stunt the mental growth and retard the education of that section of the population for whom it is the only means of communication and self-expression.

The middle-class child has access not only to a 'restricted code' (intimate family language or peer-group language) but also to Bernstein's 'elaborated code' and its speech model in his home and school environments: features – accurate grammatical order and syntax; grammatically complex sentence-structure, with conjunctions and subordinate clauses; discriminative selection from a wide range of adjectives and adverbs; inherent capability of verbalizing abstractions, etc.

9

There is a continuum, of course, from 'public' to 'formal' language. It is a matter of tendency; the lower working-class child is oriented to the 'restricted code', the middle-class to the 'elaborated'. (Bernstein stresses that it is not a matter of intelligence; some of the former class are of higher intelligence, measured by a non-verbal I.Q. rather than a verbal, some of the latter of only moderate intelligence.)

A sample of the 'restricted' code in use:

'Well it should do but it don't seem to nowadays, like there's still murders going on now, any minute now or something like that they get people don't care they might get away with it then they all try it and it might leak out one might tell his mates that he's killed someone it might leak out like it might get around he gets hung for it like that.'

Age 17. I.Q. Verbal 99; Non-verbal 126+.
(From a transcript of a recorded discussion)

The nation's need for 'spoken literacy' is far greater than its need for good voice-production, Received Pronunciation, or any other forms or aspects of an 'acceptable' accent.

The individual also needs 'spoken literacy'; and *beyond* this the greatest power of language of which he is capable – we may call this 'articulacy'. He must use language in order to learn to think. The development of language and the development of the power of thought go together and react upon each other. If he is to fulfil his intellectual potential the child needs the power of language. Education in speech and writing should help the individual to learn to think. Thinking effectively is one of the goals of education: hence the need for stress on the logical organization of ideas and their clear statement and on the knowledge of what constitutes proof. The child also needs language to enable him to find and hold his place in society. To qualify for responsibility whether as foreman, overseer, manager, executive, he needs the power to speak tolerably fluently and accurately in simple straightforward English.

He has other speech needs as well – the need for language experience which will educate his emotions and develop his personality through imaginative prose, sensuous poetry and liberating drama of all kinds. This language experience must come through the mouth and the ear as well as through the eyes.

The home may help him to develop his linguistic powers; very often it does not. Of all the other agencies which help to prepare the child for adult life the school is by far the most important. It is the focal socializing agency.[8] On the school rests the major burden of responsibility for the linguistic development of its children. Bernstein has shown the difficulties in the path of this development that confront the school and the child oriented to the 'public' language as he moves through the secondary school. The problem, as he sees it, is to preserve for the speaker the aesthetic and dignity which inheres in the 'public' language, its powerful forthrightness and vitality, but to make available the possibilities inherent in a 'formal' language. There are two means by which this change might be brought about, one by modification of the social structure, the other by operating directly on the speech itself. If the latter is attempted, says Bernstein, an appreciation of the difficulties involved for the lower-class pupil in the process of linguistic change cannot be too strongly emphasized. It would seem that a change in this mode of language usage involves the whole personality of the individual, the very character of his social relationships, his points of emotional and logical reference, and his conception of himself.[1, 2] We can believe, with Newsom, that experiment in teaching techniques, based on the findings of research, is needed.[6] However, according to Bernstein, under the most hopeful circumstances the educational process increases the risk of the speaker's alienation from his origins.[2] A study of Bernstein's writings is suggested.

REFERENCES

1. BERNSTEIN, B. 'Social Structure, Language and Learning.' *Educational Research*, 3, 1961, 163–76.
2. BERNSTEIN, B. 'Social Class and Linguistic Development: A Theory of Social Learning.' Ch. 24 in *Education, Economy and*

Society, ed. Halsey, A. H., Floud, J. and Anderson, C. A. The Free Press of Glencoe, New York, 1963.

3. LEWIS, M. M. *Language in Society.* Harrap, London, 1951.
4. LEWIS, M. M. *The Importance of Illiteracy.* Harrap, London, 1953.
5. MCNAIR REPORT. Report of the Committee appointed by the President of the Board of Education to consider the Supply, Recruitment and Training of Teachers and Youth Leaders, H.M.S.O., 1944.
6. NEWSOM REPORT. *Half Our Future:* A Report of the Central Advisory Council for Education (England), H.M.S.O., London, 1963.
7. NORWOOD REPORT. *Curriculum and Examinations in Secondary Schools,* H.M.S.O., London, 1943.
8. PARSONS, T. 'The School Class as a Social System.' Ch. 31 in *Education, Economy and Society*, ed Halsey, A. H., Floud, J., and Anderson, C. A., The Free Press of Glencoe, New York, 1963.

CHAPTER 3

Speech Education

The attempt to satisfy the needs

It has been suggested that the main aim in the training in spoken English to be given to children in school is the development of their powers of oral expression. They need as full a command as they can compass of that form of language behaviour we call speech. When we come to consider the promotion of articulacy it is as well to ask ourselves what are the functions of speech. What do we use spoken English for? If we can be clear about this we shall perhaps have a clearer idea of what ought to be done in school.

It is perhaps convenient at this point to make the distinction between speech and language, a distinction clearly made by linguists. Speech is the activity, a form of human behaviour – the actual meaningful making of speech sounds as daily behaviour; language is the institution, the linguistic store, words and their arrangements, catalogued in dictionaries and displayed in action in books and newspapers, and stored away in the memory of individuals, to be recalled for use in daily speech. Speech is a form of language in action.

Another form of language in action is that used in thinking. This use of silent speech may range in complexity from the idle formulation of ideas at a very simple level as one sits in a train carelessly looking out of the window to the concentrated thinking out of a problem at a high order of abstraction. Bernstein has pointed out that linguistic deprivation inhibits the development of the power to think in abstract terms.[2]

It might be thought that the use of inner speech for thought does not involve a speaker-listener relationship. Gallie, following out an argument of the nineteenth-century philosopher, Peirce, asserts that we see ourselves, as others do, through our own speech and the rest of our interpretable behaviour; and we see others (as they see themselves) through their speech and other interpretable behaviour. The important consequence is that our knowledge of our own thoughts, and hence the possibility of our controlling, developing, and criticizing them, is not essentially different from our knowledge of, and hence our power to influence, the thoughts of others. In other words, whenever we think we are in effect communicating – seeking to persuade or instruct or perhaps simply questioning – either covertly with ourselves or overtly with other people. He quotes Peirce, 'All thinking is dialogic in form. Your self of one instant appeals to your deeper self for his assent'; and again, 'One's thoughts are what he is saying to himself', that is, saying to that other self that is just coming into life in the flow of time. When one reasons it is that critical self that one is trying to persuade; and all thought whatsoever is a sign, and is mostly in the nature of language.[4]

A definitely non-communicative use of speech is the sudden outburst of pent-up feeling expressed in swearing or obscenity or a cry of happiness, joy, anger or despair. This is an emotional release, not requiring a listener. Hayakawa has pointed out that the stronger verbal taboos (e.g. those to do with sex or religion) have a genuine social value as expressions of anger. Harmless verbal substitutes for going berserk and smashing furniture, they act as a safety-valve in moments of crisis.[5]

The most important use of speech deliberately made audible is as a means of communication between human beings. Human speech is the cement of society. M. M. Lewis has pointed out that when we think of speech we think of the community.[7] Speech and people are necessary to us all. (Think of a women's tea-party or a group of men at the pub or the club. Think of the punishment inflicted by children and trade unionists on those they intend to hurt, 'sending to Coventry'. Think also of the punishment we still inflict in our prisons –

solitary confinement.) Speech is a social phenomenon. We use it to get in touch with our fellow-men at many levels; at one, for example, just to reassure ourselves that we belong to our group or to express our solidarity with the group (as when we make trivial conversation);* at a more complicated level to persuade an individual or a crowd of individuals to think in a particular way or to take some particular course of action. Speech in fact is the prime form of communication.

We communicate for various purposes. One is to inform. The more exact and precise we are in our choice of language the more clearly we inform. The most exact and precise use of language is that of science, which aims at uniqueness of reference. It is an ideal of science and logic to use words which mean exactly the same thing to everyone using them (an unattainable ideal since the user and the hearer of a word have had different individual experiences from which their meanings have been built up). The scientific use of language will (except in a sense to be referred to later) exclude feeling and emotion.

'To inform' includes 'to instruct'. Good instruction suggests exactness and precision of language usage.

The informative use of language is to be contrasted with its affective use, which is the expressive use of language to *affect* the listener, i.e. to affect his feelings. A major use to which we put speech is to influence people, to arouse in them particular responses, to create mental states.† Above all, we speak to persuade. Words and language-structure serve this end. So do voice and bodily presence. The language of the poet, the language of the politician,

* The result of what Meerloo calls 'chatterneed'.[8]

† This is particularly noticeable in the field of political discussion, where such politico-emotive words as 'party member, communist, politician' arouse both informative and affective connotations simultaneously. Words like this often communicate a fact and a judgement on the fact.[5] A politician, for example, can be to many people 'a person engaged for a large part of his working time in practical politics (a Member of Parliament, perhaps)' and, at the same time, 'a deceiver, a trickster, a spellbinder with words, one to be distrusted; one who is likely to have a double standard of behaviour in his use of language, a higher standard for private life and a lower for public'.

15

the language of the lover and the language of the advertiser are all affective. The prince of persuaders was Mark Antony.

There is also the aesthetic use of speech, the use of spoken words for the sheer delight of speaking and listening – an artistic delight in sound and sense, whether of one's own creation or of a poet's or a dramatist's or a prose writer's. The act of speaking may not be one of communication with a listener; it may be simply for the private joy of the speaker.

We can think of communication in terms of *meaning*. It is obvious from these brief glances at the informative and affective aspects of language that we use language to express and elicit meanings. We shall consider the problem of meaning later.

These are the uses to which human beings put human speech. Owing to the linguistic poverty of their homes some children exercise only a few of these uses and these at a low level of sophistication. If nothing is done at school there will be little linguistic development, and in the stations in adult life to which their talents call them the children will feel little need for an 'elaborated' code and a full set of speech uses. Thus they may be unable to take advantage of the opportunities that may come their way in life. It is clear that it is necessary to help children in school to become as skilled in these speech uses as they are capable of becoming. This training is funda-mental to personal development and social competence. It is the key which unlocks the door of opportunity in the adult world of jobs and job-responsibility. The Newsom Report stresses that personal and social adequacy depends on being articulate – that is, on having the words and language structures with which to think, to communicate what is thought, and to understand what is heard and read. [9]

We have noted that the most important use of speech is as a means of human communication. The commonest speech relationship is that of conversation. (Conversation, says Meerloo, is every man's daily share of creative activity.) [8] Perhaps there is not much the school can do directly about children's ordinary conversation except to ensure that in school it is reasonably polite and shows

16

respect for the other man's point of view. Indirectly it can be influenced by the widening of the horizon of children's ideas and the development of their language structures. But much conversation is conversation with a purpose, devoted to some ideal or practical end; it then becomes *discussion* and a worth-while school activity. Almost all school subjects lend themselves at some point during the school week to discussion, discussion guided by the teacher towards the solution of some problem – a scientific experiment, for example, or the equipping of a domestic kitchen to the best advantage or the proper care of school pets or other animals. The Newsom Report, urging that every opportunity should be seized for discussion *in every subject*, points out that discussion should be genuine, not mere testing by the teacher's question and the pupil's answer.[9] It is possible, however, to make *discussion* the main aim of a lesson, say an English lesson. A large class can be broken down into groups of five or six individuals, each with its own subject for discussion. (Children who in a large class remain tongue-tied tend to talk in a small group.) Each group, using committee procedure, should have its secretary and chairman with a weekly alternation of roles. Each secretary reports to the whole class on the work done in his group. This work helps a child to develop the ability to talk logically and consecutively, to state a case, develop a theme and propose a conclusion. Subjects for discussion can range from those based on children's experiences in home, school and neighbourhood to grander themes concerned with the larger world suggested by the reading of newspapers, magazines and books and sitting down to radio and television.

Discussion can with advantage be dramatized. The range of the roles the children play in real life can be extended at second-hand by improvisation of all kinds calling for linguistic experiment; a child can take in succession the part of the patient at the doctor's (or dentist's) and the part of the doctor (or dentist), the part of the applicant for a job and that of the interviewing employer, the part of the customer in a juke-box snack-bar and that of the proprietor of the establishment. Historical events can form the basis of improvisation, e.g. the discussion at the conference-table leading to the signing of a treaty in a period being studied, e.g. The Treaty of Paris 1763 (each child, properly briefed, representing a particular country). Situations of these kinds can be graded in difficulty so that there is the possibility of the use of a growing complexity of language. Role-playing can be an important aid to the development of a child's linguistic ability.

We have seen that two of the most important uses of language are the informative and the affective. It is important that children understand these two major uses and have plenty of practice in them, both speaking and listening. It must, however, be stressed that these are not independent categories. Often when a speaker is persuading he is informing (even if wrongly); and when he is informing he is affecting his audience (whether pleasantly or unpleasantly). When spoken language is used for communication for any purpose the speaker is intending to make an impression upon his audience, whether one person or a group in conversation or the larger gathering in the formal speech-making situation. The speaker, once he has started to speak, has to persuade his audience to go on listening to him. Even if he is using the unemotive language of science there will be an element of affect in his use of hands, eyes, body, of vocal tone and tune, of pace, pause, emphasis and volume.

We can consider affect in another, and perhaps more useful way, and think of it as residing in the listener. Whether a speaker is addressing an audience primarily to inform or to persuade he must take account of its nature and composition. American writers on speaking-in-public stress the importance of audience-analysis. The speaker, they say, must if possible find out before he speaks what sort of people he is talking to. What in content and style of delivery evokes response (emotional or other) from one listener may not from another; he must understand *his* audience.

With this important qualification we can say that to the extent that spoken language is being used exactly and precisely it is being used 'scientifically'. Practice in the informative/scientific use of language can be of two kinds. Teacher and children can read aloud individually to the class interesting prose passages of simple scientific writing (such as are to be found in Jeffares and Davies' *The Scientific Background: A Prose Anthology*)[6] or of other informative sorts of writing. They should be read straightforwardly with a sense of communication; that is to say, the reader will have a sense of reading *to* the audience, which will mean that he will from time to time look *at* different sections of the class. The fact that the reading has no affective content will not mean that the reader is inhibited from using that variety of pace, pause, phrasing and intonation that the listening ear requires if it is to be persuaded to go on listening. This variety is necessary and we have seen it will have, *must* have, the quality of affect. The material and the style of reading should both be examined by teacher and class, the former so that the particular elements of the scientific use of language shall be noted, the latter to examine the delivery of the reader and to discover how it was done so well or how it might have been better done. The second kind of practice can be found in the individual talk, given by pupil to class in a 'scientific' presentation. The talk will be aimed at informing the audience (perhaps instructing them by way of explaining a process or activity); its points will be simply and clearly made, its argument logically developed, and its delivery clear, accurate and precise. One of the strongest incentives to good speech is to have to inform those who really are uninformed.

In the scientific use of language words in running discourse are the most important element in the total presentation. In the affective use of language the actual words are not fundamental to the meaning that is intended to be conveyed; they are not the most significant element in the total act of speaking. The emotional colouring of the voice, the manipulation of intonation patterns, subtleties of rate of speaking, of pause, of emphasis, of shift of volume, the use of visual cues (movements of the hands, face, eyes, body) can enormously reinforce the literal meaning of the words, alter it, distort it, empty it of value or deliberately convey a meaning exactly the opposite. Any act of speaking in public (i.e. when the listener can see and hear the speaker) involves the interrelation of the two major sensory modalities, sight and hearing, the former supporting, or reacting destructively upon, the latter. Further, words themselves can be bearers of feeling (pleasant or unpleasant, e.g. honey, sugar, love, duck; nigger, darky, jew boy, dago, wog, wop, hun, homo, politician, gent – all these used of people. And elocution, propaganda, 'local politics' – at one time, even 'peace'). But the feeling suggested to some people may be strong, to others weak, and to others no feeling may be suggested at all. Hayakawa says that in the west and south-west of the U.S.A. polite people and newspapers have stopped using the word 'Mexican' altogether, using the term 'Spanish-speaking person' instead. 'Jap' in California has such a contemptuous connotation that one elderly woman living in Chicago always feels deeply insulted by the use of the word. Even the word 'niggardly' has to be avoided in speaking to some Negro audiences.[5] The writer was recently surprised that one of his students – an Egyptian – objected to his speaking of him as a 'foreigner'. He said that to him the word spoken by an Englishman (although there was nothing of affect – so far as the speaker was concerned – in voice, tone or manner) had something in it of contempt. When asked what word bearing no feeling for him could be used he suggested 'overseas student'. Some British educationists use the term 'less able children' instead of 'secondary modern children' – because of the suggestion of affect.

All this suggests two things: (1) That affect resides not so much in words themselves, but rather in speaker and listener – sometimes in the speaker, sometimes in the listener and sometimes in both. The meaning of words changes from speaker to speaker, from listener to listener, and from context to context. (2) That speakers should attempt to understand their audiences, whether one person or a large number, to know something of their background, and so of their biases and prejudices, and thus be able to attempt communication that is not likely to be vitiated by this sort of language difficulty.

It is important that children should be aware of the way in which language is used affectively. A start could be made with an examination of the crudest form of affective speaking, one with which most children are familiar – sarcasm. They might go on to attempt the expression of various feelings (perhaps set in the form of brief dramatic improvisations) – anger, contempt, disgust – cruder ones first, more subtle later on, and with the aid of a tape-recorder, estimate their success in achieving what they had attempted. Successful attempts could be examined to see just how the effect upon the listener was produced. It might be found that voice-quality, intonation pattern, pause, emphasis, facial expression, affective words or phrases, even the structure of the sentences, all might be involved. It is important that children should learn to use language to influence and persuade; in doing so they may learn to be on their guard against attempts to influence and persuade *them* – by advertising, for example. In the words of the Newsom Report, 'having learned in some degree how to handle words the pupils have to be helped to learn how not to be handled by them'.[9]

Alongside this practical work could go a study of the professionals' use of language. An examination of television speaking, especially advertising, can be very revealing. What are the announcer, the sports commentator, the politician, the advertiser, the pop-singer, the 'schools' lecturer or teacher, trying to do and how are they doing it? What emotions and aspirations are advertisers appealing to, and how do they play on these feelings? (Is there a moral problem here?)

The material available for reading and speaking in the education of children in the affective use of language is wider in scope than the 'scientific' material available: prose of various kinds (good examples are to be found in Sansom's *By Word of Mouth*),[10] lyrical poetry, dramatic extracts, famous speeches of exhortation or persuasion. In these forms of reading and speaking the flexibility of the voice is obviously of great importance.

It is clearly necessary that children should practise singly or in groups affective language of their own invention. Singly in the talk given to the class aimed, for example, at persuading them to think in a certain way or to follow, or refrain from, some course of action (e.g. to take up a hobby the speaker finds enjoyable, to support a charity he considers to be deserving, to vote for him in a class election, to believe in ghosts, not to take birds' eggs from a nest, not to eat broiler-farm poultry, etc.); in groups in improvisations of all kinds. The composition and delivery of television advertisements, sports commentaries and news broadcasts provide opportunities for practice in the informative and affective use of language and the creative exercise of the imagination.

Another use of language is as a source of aesthetic pleasure. Some people use spoken words for the sheer delight of using them (experiencing a sensuous pleasure in the sounds, the patterning of the words, the kinaesthetic sensations, and perhaps the meaning). Many Welsh and Irish people are fond of using language in this way. (The radio play, *Under Milkwood*, springs immediately to mind.) A great many children, perhaps the majority, are capable of responding sympathetically to language so used, deriving the keenest enjoyment from listening and speaking. The opportunity of such enjoyment should at least be offered to all children. Speech is an art as well as a tool. Language experience as an art form is a necessary part of an adolescent's education: sometimes in listening to the teacher reading prose or poetry, or to gramophone records or the radio, sometimes in interpretative reading aloud himself; sometimes taking part in a play or an extract from a play, sometimes creating with others his own improvised drama in mime, movement and speech. Adolescents need language not only as a means to the development of their power of thought and as a key to society and the world of work, but also as a means of satisfying deep personal needs, as a means of self-expression through the release of the imagination. Most adolescents are reluctant to give their emotions personal expression, but will willingly attempt to express them indirectly. They need exciting drama, sensuous poetry, compelling prose. They need the thriller, the ballad set to music (e.g. Charles Parker's modern B.B.C. ballads), their own improvised drama. These things are not only means to the flowering of personality, they are positive elements in the development of articulacy.

Reference has already been made to a major function of language: we use language to express and elicit meanings. It is apparent that meanings reside not so much in words as in people. Meanings are personal and differ from individual to individual; they are a function of personal experience.[1] Fry puts the matter clearly. The most

22

practically useful view of meaning, he says, is that for every individual at a given moment the meaning of any term is the sum of his
associations with that term. This sum naturally is the result of his
previous experience, and in succeeding moments it may be increased by further experience. If we wanted to represent this fact
graphically we might say that the meaning of a term for a given
individual is an area (representing the sum of his associations) and
that this area may be modified by subsequent events. If we now
consider the meaning of a term for two individuals we can say that
for each it is an area and that the two areas will show varying degrees of overlap according to the nature of the term and the background of the individuals. It is, in fact, by virtue of this overlap –
this community of associations – presumably, that we are able to use
language at all.[3] It is clear that the possibilities of misunderstanding
in human communication are endless – that they are particularly
likely to present a problem in the classroom. Children should be
aware of the problems of meaning.

Communication by means of speech implies a listener. American
educationists regard *Listening* as one of the fundamental communication skills. It is also a social art. Practice in listening in school should
be of many kinds and for several purposes, e.g. to discriminate
between speech sounds (a form of ear-training), to isolate and recognize the elements of an act of speech, to perceive particular examples
of the affective use of speech, to criticize constructively the way in
which a class-member has given a talk or read a passage of prose
aloud or spoken a poem, to analyse the development of the theme
of an original talk by a class-member and so to be able to make a
helpful criticism. Children need to develop the proper criteria in
these intensive activities of perception, recognition, discrimination
and criticism; here the teacher is the major formative influence.
Listening should be sharpened and the ability to listen selectively
fostered.

This sort of clinical listening can be used to good effect in the
consideration of 'accent' and dialect. An impersonal approach is
needed if the sympathetic interest of children is to be awakened and
sustained, an approach that can be made through gramophone

records of 'accent' and dialect, notably those of the British Drama League. The problem of 'standard' English and regional spoken English can be brought painlessly into the open.

'Accent' may be described as the total effect produced in the listener by a blending of the regional, the social and the personal in pronunciation, intonation, vocal quality, enunciation, pace and rhythm of speech. Where the speech climate in a school is good, i.e. where the majority of the teachers, and at least a substantial minority of the pupils, speak well and the attitude on the part of all in the school to speech and work in spoken English is sympathetic, much is done by the force of example, and the general quality of the accent of those below the prevailing level is raised without much positive action. Where the speech climate is not good the modification of accent is a very difficult undertaking. Apart from the training of the ear and the persuading of the children to adopt and consolidate new speech habits, there is often a psychological barrier in the way of remedial treatment. Any attempt at modification of accent may be felt as a threat to the individual's security, an adverse criticism of his home and upbringing, an affirmation of his inferior social class status.

This is not to say that nothing should be done. Where communication suffers it can be made obvious to children (perhaps by means of a tape-recorder) that it is worth while taking steps to improve it. Slight modification in the making of vowel sounds (away from extreme regional shaping), clearer articulation of consonants, better voice production, a more varied intonation and vocal tone, a flexible use of pace and emphasis; some or all of these may be seen by the children (with the teacher's help) to be necessary technical devices for improvement. With proper motivation a great deal can be done.

It has been suggested that the task of the school in speech education is to promote (1) the articulacy (2) the personal development and social effectiveness of its pupils, and lines of approach to the problem have been proposed. This chapter will end with a few (perhaps unanswerable) questions. Can anything more precise be done in the way of positive teaching to the end of good speaking?

Perhaps it is not necessary for the brightest and most socially competent. For all others some measure of more positive teaching seems to be necessary, even for those oriented to Bernstein's 'elaborated' code. Can they be taught scientifically to embody in their speaking the characteristic features of this code – variety of sentence-length, the weaving of subordinates into statement, question, instruction and request, the enrichment of speech with other than the most ordinary and colourless adjectival and adverbial forms, the holding of a formal subject through a speech sequence (bearing in mind the ages at which these features might be expected to appear in the language of ordinary children in non-deprived homes)? For many children it is a social problem as well as a linguistic one. Can the classroom be turned into a social/linguistic laboratory providing the proper background and techniques? Can the school bring to bear those forces of socialization which may gradually induce the use of a wider, freer code of speech which is truly developmental? Is the comprehensive school, with its apparently classless society, a better agent for this purpose than other types of secondary school?

REFERENCES

1. BERLO, D. K. *The Process of Communication.* Holt, Rinehart and Winston, London, 1960.
2. BERNSTEIN, B. 'Social Structure, Language and Learning.' *Educational Research*, 3, 1961, 163–76.
3. FRY, D. B. 'The Experimental Study of Speech.' Ch. VIII in *Studies in Communication*, ed. Evans, I., Secker and Warburg, London, 1955.
4. GALLIE, W. B. *Peirce and Pragmatism.* Pelican, 1952.
5. HAYAKAWA, S. *Language in Thought and Action.* Allen and Unwin, London, 1964.
6. JEFFARES, A. N. and DAVIES, M. B. *The Scientific Background: A Prose Anthology.* Pitman, London, 1958.
7. LEWIS, M. M. *Language in Society.* Harrap, London, 1951.

8. MEERLOO, J. A. M. *Conversation and Communication*. International Universities Press, New York, 1952.
9. NEWSOM REPORT. *Half Our Future:* A Report of the Central Advisory Council for Education (England). H.M.S.O., London, 1963.
10. SANSOM, C. *By Word of Mouth: An Anthology of Prose for Reading Aloud*. Methuen, London, 1950.

PART II

Examinations in Oral English

The testing of achievement

CHAPTER 4

Introduction

We can now attempt to answer the question: what do we want to test? The answer is clear. (1) We want a test of articulacy: a test of the candidate's ability to make a statement clearly, to state a case, to develop a theme, to rebut an argument, to persuade, to inform. It will be a test of his range and use of vocabulary, of his ability to talk coherently, lucidly and logically, a test of his power of communication, of his ability to create his own patterns of language, a test of his audibility and intelligibility. (2) We want a test of his ability to present the language of others (whether in prose, poetry or drama), to interpret the poet or dramatist or prose-writer to his audience, to 'trigger off' in the minds of his hearers a recreation of meaning and mood so that writer, speaker and listeners through the medium of spoken language are for the moment in communion one with another. In both kinds of test he will use his voice and body (including face, hands, eyes), his thought and language. In the first type of test he will use language of his own creation, in the second the language of others.

Can we test those things by looking at him and listening to him and making judgements about what we see and hear? We can – under certain conditions. We must be careful in our choice of examiners,* of the items of spoken English (perhaps Prose Reading or Poetry Speaking or the giving of a Talk, for example) we select as our vehicles of examination, of the material we choose, and of methods we employ to test the candidate.

---

* The conduct of examinations in Oral English by the non-specialist teacher will be discussed in later chapters.

American research and that of the writer has shown that the most important element in the test is the examiner (most important in the sense that, as a first requirement, we want the test to result in an accurate assessment of the candidate's ability in spoken English), and this brings us up against a fundamental difficulty – that of standardization. We want to design the test and conduct it in such a way that *any* competent examiner will, *as nearly as possible*, get the same results with any one set of candidates as any other competent examiner. Our ideal is an identity of judgement between any number of assessors judging the same set of candidates. If we were to compare two such sets of assessments we would like to see a correlation r (product-moment) of $+ 1 \cdot 00$. (This would not mean that if we were marking, say, on a scale 0–10 the two mark lists would be the same. One examiner might mark very much more leniently – his marks would be higher; but they would be *consistently* higher. The two assessors would, in fact, have exactly similar rankings.) If we knew this to be generally the case we could say then that it would not matter which examiner assessed Johnny, so long as the judge knew his job. Unfortunately it is not generally the case and it does matter very much to Johnny which judge chance happens to allot him. It is likely that the measure of agreement between any two competent examiners concerning any one set of candidates can be represented by a correlation coefficient r of about $+ 0 \cdot 75$.[2] What does this mean? Let us suppose that the top 75 per cent of candidates in an oral English test are regarded as passing (a possible state of affairs). Then we can prepare a contingency table[1] showing the relationship between the assessments of any two markers.

The reliability coefficient of a test is an estimate of how much test results may vary if the testing is repeated. The table states this estimate clearly. It suggests that there will be misclassification to the extent that (there being 100 candidates) of Marker A's pass-list of 75, Marker B would fail 9; and of Marker B's pass-list of 75, A would fail 9. Thus, of an entry list for a test in oral English of 100 candidates, $9 + 9 = 18$ will be misclassified.

Before laymen jump to the conclusion that examinations in oral

CONTINGENCY TABLE SHOWING THE RELATIONSHIP BETWEEN
THE ASSESSMENTS OF ANY TWO MARKERS $(r = 0.75)$

		MARKER B		
		Top 75%	Lower 25%	
MARKER A	Top 75%	66	9	75
	Lower 25%	9	16	25
		75	25	100

English are so much a matter of chance as to be practically worthless it must be pointed out that the degree of chance in the marking of written essay-type answers (in English or Geography, for example) is just about the same. In fact, Oral English tests are just about as reliable as written English tests. It is always possible to increase the reliability of the test, i.e. to reduce the probability of the 18 per cent misclassification noted above to a lower percentage, by using two examiners, or better still three, at any one test, and pooling their marks. There are, however, a few difficulties about this: (1) It is more expensive if the judges are paid. (2) In a two- or three-judge test the degree of strain felt by some children will be little increased if the number of judges is augmented, while in the case of others the nervous strain may be considerably greater, with a possible widening of the gap between their actual and potential performance. (3) If in a two- or three-judge test, only one assessor conducts the examination he is an observer-participant while the other one or two are merely observers. The psychological approaches to the test-situation are different and may be reflected in the differing grades or marks awarded.

Why is this ideal r of $+ 1.00$, this total community of judgement, practically unattainable? This is the question we must now attempt to answer.

REFERENCES

1. DANIELS, J. C. 'The Interpretation of Correlations.' *Bulletin of the University of Nottingham Institute of Education*, 7, 1951.
2. HITCHMAN, P. J. 'The Testing of Spoken English: A Review of Research.' *Educational Research, November*, 1964.

CHAPTER 5   *Why Judges Disagree*

I. THE TEST PERFORMANCE AND THE PROBLEM OF STANDARDS

The human brain functions by making comparisons. Every individual faced with a particular situation, deals with it by comparison with other situations through which he has passed, which have left their imprint on the memory system of the brain. Each new situation is matched by this memory system, until an adequate response is produced.[29]

Almost everybody every day makes judgements concerning people they meet for the first time. The first judgement is probably based on clothes, the second on voice and speech. Speech offers us clues by means of which we assess the new-comer. When the stranger opens his mouth he pours out a stream of information about himself, the 'clues' he offers being interpreted in different ways by different people. For assessment everybody will have his own set of criteria, acknowledged or, more probably, unacknowledged, based on experience, environmental influences and prejudice. These will enable him to form his judgements about place of origin, occupation, social class, temperament and character, engender an attitude towards the stranger and suggest to him the means of handling the new situation. This proneness to the formation of judgements based on 'clues' presented by the voice and speech of strangers, which are referred back mentally to past situations and matched up by the memory system, is 'built-in' to most of us. This referral back and matching up until an adequate response is produced is, as Young (quoted above) has shown, a natural thing to do, a natural form of behaviour.

It comes 'naturally' then to human beings to assess other human beings whom they meet for the first time on their voice and speech. It is natural also that the sets of criteria employed by any large cross-section of the population are many and enormously wide-ranging in content. When it comes to judging spoken English professionally some standardization of criteria which are to be the basis of judgement is necessary.

Even with this standardization, why is it that two examiners of equal competence are quite likely to produce very different assessments in spoken English for the same candidate? The answer seems to be that (a) judges do not perceive the same things, and (b) they evaluate what they do perceive in different ways.[20] It is worth while looking at this problem rather closely. To do so we must look at the Test performance and the people involved in it, and at the Test itself and the conditions in which it is conducted.

Let us look, for example, at a test of the candidate's ability to speak a poem or to read aloud a passage of prose, or to give a talk.

(i) *The Test Performance*

Each performance is made up of primary constituents, which are inherent in the performance, and secondary constituents, which are 'given' by the individual assessor.

The primary constituents are physical facts, objectively measurable. They include speed of speaking or reading, range of pitch, intonation or 'tune' patterns, pauses which may vary considerably in length, degree of stress on syllables, force or intensity of voice. Even the timbre or quality of voice is analysable by mechanical and electro-acoustic techniques. These are physical facts of a speaking performance which remain the same in measurement whether an examiner is present or absent, or indeed whether the speaker is present or absent, since his speaking performance can be given – as far as these aspects of it are concerned – by a machine.

These facts are objectively measurable, but as far as tests in spoken English for schools and colleges are concerned, they are not worth measuring. In the first place the difficulties and costs of administration would be prohibitive, and in the second, a human judgement would still be necessary to decide whether, in context, these facts, contributing to a perceived whole, were 'good', 'bad', or 'indifferent'. The truth is that vocal expression can be measured by only one standard – *its effect upon listeners*. As one American speech expert has put it, 'Vocal expression is something to be perceived, something to be reacted to, and if we would appraise it we must do so by measuring the reactions of listeners.'[25]

There are also inherent in the speaking performance some primary constituents which are not objectively measurable. These include elements representative of the personality of the candidate – his stance, facial expression, gesture; in Hazlitt's words, 'the speaking eye, the conscious attitude . . . all those brave sublunary things that make his raptures clear. . . .' Professor Pear has put it more prosaically, 'The aesthetic unsatisfactoriness of a telephone conversation suggests that most of us, when face to face, watch the speaker and freely interpret changes of facial expression and coloration, of posture and gesture.'[14] We must also include in the primary constituents not objectively measurable the quality and style of the prose read and of the poems spoken, i.e. of the material, which is as much a part of the speaking performance as the speaker is.

The Test performance in spoken English is also made up of secondary constituents contributed by the mind of the assessor, himself influenced by his physical and emotional state: qualities 'given' to the performance by the assessor's liking or disliking of the candidate's timbre of voice (created by the past experience of the listener and the effect of the timbre upon him in this context), of the prose, the poem, the subject for the talk, 'given' to the performance by the assessor's interpretative activities (influenced by his personal feelings), by prejudice, by habit of mind, experience, education, training, mental 'set', motivation, personality.

An American experimenter has spoken of the 'performance-as-given' as distinct from the 'performance-as-perceived'. He suggests that there is a 'correct' performance which is free from the 'interpretative' activities of the perceiver. He quotes an American philosopher, Oliver Martin: 'What is given to us in perception are never "wild" data. The given is just what it is, always perfectly innocent of the crime of error.'[20] In the case of our speaking performance the 'given' amounts to no more than the objectively measurable 'facts' already noted: noises, speeds, lengths of silence, intensities, movements. It is the observer who takes these things and by fusing them with what he himself can 'give' creates the 'performance'. As Ayer has said: 'The famous distinction which Locke drew between primary and secondary qualities is not a distinction between those perceived qualities that are unaffected by the conditions of observation and those that are affected. Since all are affected there is no such distinction, as Berkeley realized.'[2] An 'objective performance' does not, in fact, exist; at least, a 'performance-as-given' is no more than a meaningless jumble of noises, silences and movements. And for each observer there is an individual 'performance-as-perceived'. There are exactly as many performances as there are observers.

(ii) *'Knowing'*, *Interpreting and Judging the Performance*

The assessor's 'knowledge' of the candidate's performance grows as the performance develops. Such aspects of the speaking performance as voice or power of verbal expression are not known at the beginning, then are imperfectly known, then more fully known as the speaking continues. The assessor is acquiring a growing apprehension of the candidate's performance in these details. In the meantime, as Oldfield says of the candidate in the interview, a 'permanent total apprehension (or general picture, a "General Impression") is being progressively built up outside consciousness. . . . The candidate is something which progressively becomes more and more familiar to the interviewer.'[13] In our case it is not only the candidate but also his speaking performance, through the interaction of the auditory and the visual, which becomes more familiar. The eminent psychologist Stout has said, 'A sensible appearance on which attention is persistently concentrated must in some degree suffer modification. The appearance which is distinctly known cannot remain quite the same as the appearance which is vaguely known, or merely experienced without being noticed.'[19]

Often the standard of the speaking performance does not change as the performance progresses – it is the observer (the assessor) who suffers change. The philosopher Bradley said, 'Attention is practical, but it is not practical except as altering myself and so causing the object, unaltered by me, to maintain and develop itself before me and in me.'[3] Sometimes, however, changes may be made by the candidate in his standard of speaking, perhaps as a result of growing confidence, perhaps of some instability due to nervousness or physical condition.

Observation and interpretation may be a single complex process. Is judgement bound up in this complex, or does the assessor halt on the brink of judgement, waiting until he 'knows' the performance sufficiently well for tentative judgements to be formed?

Oldfield thinks that observation and assessment go along together. He says that the process of assessment, although in general it only reaches the stage of explicit formulation at the end of the interview, is one which is continuously taking place throughout. The actual process he describes thus: there is a tendency for more or less clearly formulated *judgements* about the candidate to emerge. Every now and then the process of observation is broken into, and a 'judgement' is either deliberately made or involuntarily enters consciousness.[13] An American experimenter, Thompson, says that 'premature affirmation of the classification is reconsidered more or less automatically'.[20] Introspecting, the present writer thinks that as far as the details such as voice or power of verbal expression are concerned he makes a tentative judgement almost at once, and then a series of revisions, ending with a final considered judgement. The 'General Impressions', which have been gradually building up, crystallize into judgements at the end of each part of the test.

(iii) *The Assessment of the Performance*

Several factors tend to make assessment difficult and to cast doubt upon its reliability.

(*a*) THE COMPLEXITY OF THE SPEECH ACT. This perhaps is the cause of the primary difficulty in testing speech performance. Many variables are involved in the act of speaking. Voice alone varies in pitch, timbre and loudness, and in the pattern with which these variables change. Then there are pace of speaking (which can vary in any one speaking performance), pronunciation, diction, intonation and visible behaviour (stance, facial expression, movement, gesture). The use of language is an important variable (embodying words, sentence-structure, grammar, pause).

The speech act, while being a subtle organization of many variable elements, is yet essentially a unit. What the observer perceives is a unified whole, a fusion of the visual and the audible – a speaking performance. The interaction and fusion of the many variables in a speaking performance make their selection and isolation for the purpose of testing very difficult. Yet it is just this judging of details that many assessors are asked to undertake – quite rightly, since it is the indispensable preliminary to the making of a reliable estimate of the 'General Impression'.

The difficulty inherent in the complex nature of the act of speaking is complicated by the fleeting nature of the evidence presented to the assessor. Once given, a performance is lost and cannot be repeated.

(b) THE PROBLEM OF STANDARDS. How does a competent judge in a spoken English test set up standards so that he can discriminate satisfactorily between candidates?

In the first place he has, or should have, a set of briefing instructions which include a Rating Scale describing a set of 'standards' as objectively as possible. (Such a scale is set out in Appendix 2.) This Rating Scale should give him a clear idea of what the Test authorities consider in a speaking performance to be, say, good voice or poor voice, a high standard of verbal expression or a low one (and so on through a number of 'details' or aspects of the speaking performance). Discussion with the Chief Examiner should enable the assessors to be of one mind in this matter – as far as any group of human beings can be.

In the second place the assessor will have long-term standards of his own. Largely as a result of long practice he will have established for himself a set of absolute judgements, a natural scale of reference, an implicit and well-articulated standard.

The psychologist, M. D. Vernon, has shown that when subjects are asked to make absolute judgements of size or intensity without the use of a comparison standard the distribution of judgements seems to be based partly upon the range of stimuli which occurs in the experiment and partly upon more general and persistent impressions derived from previous experience. Describing experiments in weight-lifting she shows that there are short-term and long-term standards or 'levels' of judgement; short-term based upon weights lifted during the experiment, long-term based upon the observer's general standard of heaviness and lightness in everyday life.[24]

This exactly describes the situation in the testing of spoken English. Any particular test will compel the assessor to make discriminations between candidates at differing levels suggested by the Rating Scale. Eriksen and Hake (two experimenters in another field) say that judgements are never made in a vacuum but are always made relative to a standard or reference level that is subjectively present. The subject (in our case, the assessor), when confronted with a series of stimuli in an absolute-judgement task, selects a few stimuli in the series that he then uses as standards for judging the remaining stimuli. When a different stimulus is presented the subject attempts to recall one of these 'standard' stimuli and uses it as a reference in judging the presented stimulus. Essentially he transforms the task into a comparative judgement using the recalled value of the selected standard as the comparison stimulus.[7]

What almost certainly happens in the testing of spoken English is as follows. To help in his task of judging the assessor has a 'standard', described as objectively as possible in the Rating Scale. The assessor uses his first few cases to establish a 'standard' of judgements against which he sets succeeding examples of voice, power of verbal expression, etc. These first few stimuli serve as 'anchors'. Judgements of them are based, it seems, on a synthesis of the Rating Scale and the 'long-term standards' already present in the mind of the assessor. Then at any point in the succession of cases an example of the 'very good' or of the 'very bad' may turn up, and these too will take their places as 'anchors', to which succeeding cases may be referred.

It seems then that, where judgements of spoken English are to be made in an oral test, the assessor will, to some extent, be influenced by his 'long-term standard', and by the sort of 'short-term standard' that is to be found evolving in his judging as the work proceeds.

39

To sum up this discussion of the problem of standards we may say that the competent assessor brings his own long-term standards to the examination-room and relates the performances he sees and hears to those standards; and that, as the series of performances is presented his judgements come more and more to be a function of these particular performances, i.e. to be a series of performance-comparisons at standard-values suggested by the Rating Scale. A combination of long-term and short-term standards produces a set of considered judgements.

Different assessors may have differing 'long-term standards'. Some assessors may have difficulty in synthesizing their long-term standards with the standards of the Rating Scale. These differences may prove a major factor in the inconsistency of judgements as between assessor and assessor.

There is also a different sort of difficulty involving standards. An American experimenter, Seedorf, has pointed out that 'it is impossible to separate oral interpretation from the difficulties involved in the evaluation of any object with aesthetic appeal. . . . Since there is no perfect agreement on standards of artistic oral interpretation, and since all judges are not capable of recognizing the extent to which these standards have been attained by a given reader, the rating that a reader receives from any judge is, if not capricious, at least subject to that judge's own powers of aesthetic discrimination.'[18]

This state of unreliability among judges in evaluating an art form will affect assessments of poetry speaking and, to a lesser extent, those of prose reading. (Judgements of the speaking of passages of prose with an emotional or aesthetic appeal are much more likely to be affected than those of a factual or argumentative nature, but the presentation of even the latter does involve an aesthetic element. The total impression created in the assessor by the manipulation of voice, tone, rhythm, bodily stance, facial expression, etc., may contain suggestions of 'pleasantness' or 'unpleasantness' as well as of the degree of competence in projecting the ideas or facts in the passage; in fact, such is the unity of a speaking performance, the 'pleasantness' may be part of the 'competence'.)

A problem related to that of standards concerns the number of categories or classes which should be used in oral English examinations. The differing powers of discrimination of different assessors may be a further source of inconsistency in the making of judgements. To ask an assessor to divide a candidate-list into a greater number of classes than he really has power to discriminate is to introduce a spurious and illusory degree of refinement into assessment grading. What is the number of categories that both serves the purpose of the test and best suits the general run of assessors?

(c) THE COMPLEX NATURE OF THE EXAMINATION PROCESS. What Oldfield says of interviewing is true also of conducting an examination in spoken English. 'Skill in interviewing depends not only upon the mastery of the several activities which go to make it up, but also upon the capacity to carry them on simultaneously and to combine them in one unified performance directed to a definite purpose.'[13]

The occasion has the same sort of social nature, requiring the politeness of civilized intercourse, the lubricating talk, the pleasant manner, the setting of the candidate at ease. There are also the same concurrent activities of observation, interpretation, and assessment, with a number of judgements to be made definitely in a brief time.

2. EXAMINER AND CANDIDATE

A further complicating factor, tending to make assessment difficult and to cast doubt upon its reliability, is the intensely human situation involved in the confrontation of assessor and candidate. Here in the interplay of personality and the differing degrees of motivation will be found a major source of error in the making of judgements (that is to say, a major cause of disagreement amongst assessors).

(i) Personality

Perhaps the greatest single factor deciding the success or failure of the test is the personality of the assessor. (The test is successful if it has given a candidate a perfectly fair opportunity to reach his speech 'potential'.) In ten or fifteen minutes the examiner is asked to make honestly and carefully a series of assessments based on a set of criteria with which he has become familiar but which may to some extent conflict with his own 'long-term' standards based on his own experience. At the same time he is in a state of lively personal relationship with the candidate, a relationship which he must conduct and influence in such a way that the candidate is persuaded and helped to realize his full 'potential' speaking performance. In this brief time the candidate must be welcomed, set at his ease as far as possible, persuaded to give of his best, and ushered out gracefully. In spite of this time factor there must be no hurry; there must be no suggestion that the candidate is one of many on a conveyor-belt.

Differences in personality in assessors may be a considerable factor detracting from the reliability of tests. But the potential force of this factor is enormously increased in the interplay of personality between assessor and assessed. For the candidate also has a personality which, while of lesser importance in the testing situation than that of the assessor (since the latter almost always plays the dominant role), makes its unique contribution to the test complex. In order to know a candidate's speech the assessor must, to a certain extent, know the person. At least he knows him better at the end of the test than he did at the beginning. But his knowing him depends on the degree of rapport he has been able to build up during the course of the test. This degree will vary from couple (examiner and examined) to couple. Some assessors will be better at 'getting in touch' with candidates than others, and thus in persuading them to give a better speaking performance. Prejudice may flavour the relationship between the two parties to the test; on either side there may be feelings of dislike or active liking, of repulsion or attraction. The assessor may, in fact, overcompensate for these feelings. If there is hostility between examiner and candidate the test is bound to be a failure.

(ii) *Motivation*

It is recognized in everyday life that a person's performance on a given occasion does not always measure up to his ability. He does not run as fast or shoot as accurately or speak as convincingly as he has on other occasions. He is perhaps not highly motivated, or he may even be over-motivated

and so eager to succeed as to lose control of his resources of energy and skill.
Both ability and motivation are factors in performance, and if either of these
is entirely lacking the performance does not occur. Ability is like a machine
which cannot do its work unless power is applied.[28]

Motivation is of tremendous importance in the testing of spoken
English for it determines the nature of co-operation between assessor
and candidate. It is also a determinant of perception. Woodworth
and Schlosberg (quoted above) note two motivation factors common to both parties in the tests, candidates and assessors:[28]

(*a*) TASK-INTEREST. This covers the general interest and enjoyment
of both parties in the testing, absorption in the task as an interesting
problem (assessors), and the novelty of the experience and the desire
to know results (candidates).

(*b*) EGO-INTEREST. This factor causes the tasks to be regarded by
both parties as tests of their abilities. Each person involved wishes
to prove to himself that he can do his part of the job satisfactorily.
The challenge can produce a stimulation of effort. Morale becomes
an element in motivation.

A third factor is:

(*c*) INTEGRITY. Honesty and self-respect should lead both parties
to the test to do their best. An assessor will be inspired by ideals of
duty; but his judgement is not likely to be questioned officially and
he can be as careful or as careless as he likes. The moral factors
require the backing of systematic knowledge.

An American psychologist, Johnson, warns his readers, 'When
the going gets tough many motives are extinguished'.[10]

PERCEPTION

A major source of inconsistency between the assessments of judges
is to be found in the perceptual habits of human beings. Since these
first became the subject of study philosophers and psychologists
have argued the nature of perception. It is no part of our business
here to consider the arguments; we are concerned with the spoken
English test, the candidate and the 'perceiving' assessor. According to
Russell Brain, the great neurologist, the physical stimuli excite the
appropriate receptor organs (the eyes and the ears in our case) which

in turn start electrical impulses in the corresponding nerves running to the brain. What determines our awareness of a sensation, and also its nature, is the arrival of nerve-impulses at the appropriate end-stations of the brain. The brain-state is the last of a series of events caused by the physical stimuli. The simplest brain-event concerned with sensation never occurs in isolation. The nervous system is in constant activity, with nerve-impulses streaming in. Some of these impulses reach consciousness in the form of direct awareness; others never reach consciousness individually but contribute to the meaning of other items of consciousness. The combination of our sense organs and the nervous system when stimulated by the impact of physical impulses coming from outside has the peculiar property of creating in various ways symbolical representations of the rest of the world. The physical world is common to all observers; the perceptual representation of it is private and subjective. This perceptual world is a construct of the percipient's brain.[4,5]

It is now easy to see why assessors may disagree in their judgements of a speaking performance. There are as many perceptual worlds as there are brains in the physical world, and when a single speaker gives a performance there are as many 'performances' to be judged as there are assessors. Perception is not merely reproductive, it is *creative*.[12]

Let us consider now why the perceptual world of one assessor may differ from that of another. To begin with, Ayer has pointed out that the sense organs and brain of the observer affect the nature of what is experienced.[1] McKellar also stresses the importance of the sense organs in perception. He points out that an individual's awareness of his material and social environment, and of his own conscious processes, depends upon the integrity and functioning of his sense organs.[12] Thus the judgements that an assessor will make in a spoken English test will depend, partly, upon the state of his eyesight and of his hearing, upon his general state of health, and the degree of physical fatigue affecting his bodily state. Temporary distractions such as headache, toothache, ear-ache, may also affect his judgements.

The set of events external to the percipient (a speaking performance, for example) Oldfield calls 'perceptual cues'. There is always, he says, a selection of cues in perception. 'But if selection of cues be a characteristic of perception it follows that different percipients may select differently.'[13]

Perception is largely determined by *selectivity*, which is strongly influenced by the temperament of the assessor, his attitudes, his interests, the degree of goodwill he brings to his task, his predispositions, his experience, education, training, intelligence, skill, and by his powers of voluntary attention. These variables may be a major source of inconsistency in the making of judgements as between assessors.

It is worth while to glance at those forces in our lives which induce one assessor to make one selection of cues in perception and another to make a different selection.

(i) *Experience*

Experience helps to mould our perception and largely shapes our interpretation of what we perceive. What we know is brought to bear upon what we observe. Previous perception – what is remembered – combines with present perception to equip an individual to make judgements, to assess meaning, to classify and to solve problems.[12]

'In every field,' says McDougall, 'the expert perceives far more than the inexpert, because he reacts upon similar sense-impressions with a more adequately prepared mind. In some sense the stored traces of his many experiences in his special field of observation rise up to meet the sense-impressions and to mould them in conformity with those past experiences.'[11]

(ii) *Bias and Prejudice*

Bias and prejudice, in assessment as in the ordinary activities of daily life, are products of experience, which bring to life the orectic process of perception – feeling, emotion and impulse. It is inevitable that the minds and the experiences of assessors, as of other individuals, will prejudice them to like or dislike certain elements of presentation or, worse still, the total presentation.

Dealing with the assessment of personality, R. L. Thorndike and Hagan point out that, in some cases, our ratings of one or more traits may be affected, but that often the bias is one of general liking for or aversion to the person, and this generalized reaction colours all our specific ratings. Thus, the ratings reflect not only the general subjective rating standard of the rater, but also his specific biases with respect to the person being rated.[22] E. L. Thorndike was the first to give this 'error' the name of 'Halo Effect'. Dealing with personality and achievement ratings of officers made by their superiors in the United States Army he said, 'Obviously a halo of general merit was extended to influence the rating for the special ability or vice versa.'[21] This can very easily happen in a spoken English test. If an assessor takes an instant dislike to a candidate or is attracted by a pretty face, or likes or dislikes the voice of the candidate or the whole performance in a general way his detailed markings of separate aspects of a speaking performance may be considerably influenced by his emotional and mental state. In this case we may say that a 'Halo' is running through the marks of any one candidate; i.e. the individual marks tend to be all about the same. The influence of the Halo is a factor to be reckoned with in the judgement of speaking performances. (Conversely it is important to be on one's guard against the over-compensated Halo.)

(iii) *Education and Training*

Education and training also help to mould perception and shape interpretation of what is perceived. They are likely to impose on the assessor a 'set', or slant, which compels him to look at his job, at the candidate, and at the speaking performance in a particular way. The schools of speech and drama turn out annually scores of trained teachers, many of whom will assess speaking performances as part of their regular way of earning a living, and others of whom will do so from time to time. Some principals of strong personality impress upon their staffs and pupils their own distinctive ways of teaching and judging. Other specialists in speech and drama have received their training from private teachers, some of whom stand high in their profession and all of whom are likely to be a formative background influence on their protégés as assessors. Another type of assessor likely to become increasingly prominent is the teacher of English (who may or may not have had training in voice and speech). His (or her) education will have been very different from that of the assessor who has been trained at a school of speech and drama; it may produce a distinctive 'set' which will help to fashion his perception of the performance. The phonetician's professional training produces a very distinctive 'set' and so does the professional actor's or actress's.

Education, intelligence, aptitude and training will produce varying degrees of skill in judging that may be a contributory factor to inconsistency as between assessors in the making of judgements.

(iv) *Set*

These or some other sorts of 'mental set' produce an attitude of mind in the assessor which fashions his perception of the speaking performance. The set has a strong qualitative influence on perception, slanting the perceiver towards perception of some objects and some aspects of the environment rather than others.[10] Sometimes a 'set' is a factor necessary to the success of a test or an experiment, e.g. the observer may have to select and isolate certain features from a complex percept, observing these alone and ignoring the remainder of the field.[24] This is necessary in those tests in spoken English in which the assessor is required to isolate and judge certain elements, say, voice or power of verbal expression – taken out of the candidate's total speaking performance. Some 'sets' tend to militate against reliable assessment. 'Expectation' is a mental set that colours judgement. 'The listener who hears an excellent performance may anticipate that the rest will not be as good; similarly he who hears a series of poor speeches may think that the next cannot help being better.[20] William James said that confident expectation of a certain intensity or quality of impression will often make us sensibly see or hear it in an object which really falls far short of it.[9] Another sort of 'set', called 'habitual set', induces an assessor to refrain from immediately repeating a mark or a category of judgement. It seems that he feels impelled to change his response because of his previous response. No one can know what background 'sets' are operating in the case of a particular assessor, probably not even the assessor himself.

The afferent side of this set, the preparation for perceiving some things to the neglect of other things, often goes by the name of *attention*.[10]

(v) *Attention*

Perception is largely determined by selectivity, conscious and unconscious. Controlled attention is the means whereby the observer is able to use his powers of conscious selectivity. Voluntary control results in attention to some percepts and some ideational processes rather than others.[15] Thus the assessor can concentrate at one time on voice, at another on pronunciation, and again on, say, power of verbal expression.

The modern view of attention is that it is the activity of a human being, a person 'attending'; it is the direction of awareness, either spontaneously or voluntarily, towards different parts of the perceptual field. Psychologists distinguish two kinds of attention: (a) Involuntary (or spontaneous) attention, created by interest, and (b) Voluntary (or controlled) attention, created by the will.

(a) INVOLUNTARY ATTENTION. We attend in spite of ourselves because the stimulus is strong enough to force itself into consciousness. We are interested, and to have an 'interest' in any object is to be ready to pay attention to it. Interest is latent attention; and attention is interest in action.[11] It is likely that at the beginning of a session of spoken English testing the stimulus will be strong enough to generate in the assessor an involuntary attention.

(b) VOLUNTARY ATTENTION. A person attends when by a deliberate effort of will he pre-selects a particular field.[27] William James says that effort characterizes voluntary attention. 'There is no such thing as voluntary attention sustained for more than a few seconds at a time. What is called sustained voluntary attention is a repetition of successive efforts which bring back the topic to the mind.'[9] Woodworth and Schlosberg say that it is possible to attend to a complex object much longer than five seconds, but only by shifting from one part to another part of the object.[28] This is highly relevant to the assessor's attempt to form a 'General Impression'. It suggests that some sort of examination of 'details' must go to the formation of a General Impression. And, further, that if this is the case, then the prior making of actual 'detail' assessments should result in the making of a more 'reliable' General Impression.

Whether there is or is not some sort of examination of 'details' prior to the formation of a General Impression, such a formation comes naturally and congenially to the assessor in spoken English. The speech performance is a complex, unified whole, and as Valentine says, the mind constantly reveals a tendency to organize or integrate impressions into wholes[23] (a point emphasized by the Gestalt-psychologists).

The General Impression is a Gestalt, the whole which is more than the sum of its parts. Everyday perception yields numerous illustrations of the gestaltist's figure-ground phenomenon. (The 'figure' is the important and striking part of the field, and the 'ground' is the background provided by the remainder of the field.) For example, in a lecture the speaker's voice may be 'figure', an auditory gestalt which is perceived as segregated from a 'ground' of incidental lecture-room noises. The strength of a gestalt is the extent to which the nature of the whole determines the nature of the parts.[12] It will readily be realized that in some assessors the influence of the General Impression (Halo) upon the perception of the 'details' will be much greater than in others.

An earlier, and perhaps from our point of view more useful, way of looking at the perceptual field is to consider it in terms of 'focus' and background or 'margin' of consciousness. Valentine prefers this terminology. 'We have a clear focus, a near margin less clear, and wider background still more vague.'[23]

Thus in our testing of spoken English first one 'detail', then another, will be the focus of voluntary attention, with the others in the near margin of attention. Of these others some may subtly influence the assessor's perception of the one under consideration. Then, possibly, some attribute or other of one of the 'details' in the near margin may suddenly leap to the focus of attention – an

49

intrusive [g], a nasalized vowel, a false concord, a dialect word – the intrusion may depend on the background and prejudices of the assessor. When he considers the 'General Impression' not only the 'details' will be in the margin of attention. There will be other elements, e.g. manifestations of personality – stance, gesture, 'the speaking eye, the conscious attitude'. Then in the remote margin or background will be the room, everything in it, clock, fire, pictures, maps, and things outside, hum of traffic, noise of children, the Town Hall clock seen through the window. The effects are likely to be variable from person to person.

(vi) The Interrelation of the Senses

In our consideration of the processes by which speaking performances are perceived by assessors it is important to include a brief discussion of the interrelation of the senses. Those most obviously used are the major sensory modalities, the auditory and the visual; less obviously, the kinaesthetic. Most objects of our everyday lives are perceived by means of two or more sensory modalities working in co-operation. One usually predominates, but in most cases other senses help to fill out the total object, scene or occasion.[17] We perceive the total situation; this is what we do in everyday life, and this is what the assessor does in testing. Some authorities consider the heteromodal pairs as forming a unity or gestalt, others regard the relation as figure and ground (in a speech test the auditory would be 'figure' and the visual 'ground'). Guilford and Hackman say that the 'set' or adjustment typically found in attention usually favours one sense at a time; we look or we listen; we are eye-minded or ear-minded for the moment. We may look and listen simultaneously, but are the visual and auditory experiences together in the focal level of clearness, is there a shifting back and forth between them, or are the two at different levels of clearness?[8] Bentley insists that it is the rule and not the exception that the various forces of stimulus and the various receptorial resources co-operatively produce the object and the living scene. The most that can be credited to the single sense is a point of emphasis or focus.[17] Relations between sense-departments are very much conditioned by the past life of the observer and the development of perceiving during that life.[17] Cherry questions whether the various 'senses' are to be regarded as separate, independent detectors. The human organism, he says, is one integrated whole, stimulated into responses by physical signals; it is not to be thought of as a box, carrying various independent pairs of terminals labelled 'ears', 'eyes', 'nose', etc.[6]

Instead of co-operating one system may exert a disruptive influence upon another. Sight can inhibit hearing. A startling tie, an arresting hair-style or a pretty face may, perhaps only momentarily, distract the assessor from his attentive listening. More serious would be a mannerism in operation throughout a speaking performance – a nervous tic, an irrelevant gesture or a peculiarity of stance.

We can say of sight and hearing that one sense can enhance the effect produced by the other if it is a background, but as soon as it becomes a rival it diminishes the effect.

So far we have been dealing with perceptual factors that may lead to disagreement between assessors. There is one important non-perceptual factor; each assessor evaluates what he perceives in his own individual way. He is practising a skill, the degree of excellence of which has been reached as a result of his natural aptitude, training and practice. Intelligence and education play a part in his evaluation of a performance, but much more in the consideration of some 'details' than of others. Training and skill are more important in the assessment of voice and diction, intelligence and education in the assessment of the quality of a candidate's interpretative powers and of his power of verbal expression. In the assessment of a General Impression all these forces will be in operation, and in composition will be weighted differently from assessor to assessor.

Having examined the factors, perceptual and non-perceptual, conditioning an assessor's judgement, we must now look at some of the factors affecting a candidate's performance. Motivation has been dealt with earlier in this chapter (p. 43). Other factors which affect the performance include his physiological condition, the effect upon him of the testing procedure, his powers of concentration, and his emotional state.

By its very nature a testing situation tends to destroy the normal conditions under which a speech performance takes place. The knowledge that he is to be tested often changes the behaviour of the speaker. He may exert himself, become more tense, or depart from his 'normal' speaking performance. If he is aware of certain procedural details, such as the use of Rating Scales, the situation may become an artificial one to him. It is not unusual to observe changes in use of voice, particularly in variation and flexibility, as the speaker overcomes his initial tension in a speech and becomes better adjusted and more relaxed.[16] Pear says that the prospect of conversation – merely imagining it – may cause excitement, pleasure or 'unpleasure', or fear. The 'bodily occurrence' may be very disturbing.[14]

A candidate may enter the examination-room emotionally maladjusted to the situation, and unable to concentrate on the business in hand. He may be preoccupied with good or bad news just received, or with some exciting event soon to take place.

3. OTHER FACTORS

In addition to the sources of error that inhere in the rating process each measuring device provides sources peculiar to itself. There is, for example, the fleeting nature of the evidence. The speaking performance has to be examined at the time (or very shortly after) it is delivered. It cannot be repeated. Then there is the fact that in spite of adequate consultation Rating Scale terminology may involve differences of meaning for different assessors.

One more factor contributing to inconsistency of judgements as between assessors lies in what may be called the *external conditions* of the test. There is, first, the possibility of imperfect standardization of physical conditions. Rooms used may be very different one from another in size, shape, height, acoustic properties, furnishings and general degree of convenience and comfort, temperature, quality of lighting.

Then there may be physical distractions in the examination-room: views from the window including moving objects, noises from outside, interruptions – these may affect candidate and assessor differently as to *attention*, and may affect the *performance* of the candidate, and the *judgement* of the assessor.

SUMMARY

Each speaking performance consists of (a) primary constituents, inherent in the performance; (b) secondary constituents, 'given' by the assessor. It can be measured by only one yardstick, its effect upon listeners.

The assessor's 'knowledge' of the candidate's performance grows as the performance develops. Interacting with this knowledge are interpretation and assessment. A tentative assessment is under constant revision.

Complicating factors in the problem of assessment are: the complexity of the speech act, the question of standards, the optimum number of categories or classes, the complex nature of the examination process.

Sources of inconsistency as between assessors in the making of judgements are: (1) *in judges and candidates*: personality, motivation; (2) *in judges*: physiological factors (e.g. state of hearing, eyesight, general health, physical fatigue) and psychological factors (e.g. the determinants of selection in perception – experience, bias and prejudice, education and training, 'sets' of various kinds, attention; and the interrelation of the senses); (3) *in candidates*: physiological condition, effect on the candidate of the testing procedure, power of concentration, emotional state; (4) *in the test*: mechanical and verbal sources of error; (5) *in external conditions*: imperfect standardization of material conditions, physical distractions.

As long as we have to rely upon subjective judgement in the testing of spoken English (and there is, as yet, no reason to suppose that there will ever in the last resort be anything else to rely on) we may expect something less than the perfect consistency of judgement as between assessors. It will not be surprising if correlations of markings are substantially below $+1·00$.

REFERENCES

1. AYER. A. J. *The Foundations of Empirical Knowledge*. Macmillan, London, 1951.
2. AYER. A. J. *The Problem of Knowledge*. Macmillan, London, 1956.
3. BRADLEY, F. H. 'On Active Attention.' *Mind*, New Series XI, 1902, 1–30.
4. BRAIN, R. *Mind, Perception and Science*. Blackwell Scientific Publications, Oxford, 1951.
5. BRAIN, R. *The Nature of Experience*. The University Press, Oxford, 1959.
6. CHERRY, C. *On Human Communication*. Chapman and Hall, London, 1957.
7. ERIKSEN, C. S. and HAKE, H. W. 'Anchor Effects in Absolute Judgments.' *J. exp. Psychol.*, 53, 1957, 132–8.
8. GUILFORD, J. P. and HACKMAN, R. B. 'Varieties and Levels of Clearness correlated with Eye-Movements.' *Amer. J. Psychol.*, 48, 1936, 371–88.
9. JAMES, W. *Principles of Psychology*. Vol. I. Macmillan, London, 1890.
10. JOHNSON, D. M. *Psychology of Thought and Judgment*. Harper and Bros. New York, 1955.
11. MCDOUGALL, W. *An Outline of Psychology*. Methuen, London, 1923.
12. MCKELLAR, P. *A Textbook of Human Psychology*. Cohen and West, London, 1952.
13. OLDFIELD, R. C. *The Psychology of the Interview*. Methuen, London, 1951.
14. PEAR, T. H. *The Psychology of Conversation*. Nelson, Edinburgh, 1939.
15. PEEL, E. A. *The Psychological Bases of Education*. Oliver and Boyd, Edinburgh and London, 1960.
16. ROBINSON, K. F. *Teaching Speech in the Secondary School*. Longmans Green, New York, 1954.
17. RYAN, T. A. 'Interrelation of the Sensory Systems in Perception.' *Psychol. Bulletin*, 37, 1940, 659–98.

18. SEEDORF, E. H. 'An Experimental Study in the Amount of Agreement among Judges in evaluating Oral Interpretation.' *J. educ. Res.*, 43, 1949, 10–21.

19. STOUT, G. F. *Analytic Psychology*. Vol. I. Swan Sonnenschein, London, 1902.

20. THOMPSON, W. 'An Experimental Study of the Accuracy of Typical Speech Rating Techniques.' Unpub. thesis, North Western University, Evanston, Illinois, 1943.

21. THORNDIKE, E. L. 'A Constant Error in Psychological Ratings.' *J. appl. Psychol.*, 4, 1920, 25–9.

22. THORNDIKE, R. L. and HAGAN, E. *Measurement and Evaluation in Psychology and Education*. Chapman and Hall, London, 1955.

23. VALENTINE, C. W. *Psychology and its Bearing on Education*. Methuen, London, 1959.

24. VERNON, M. D. *A Further Study of Visual Perception*. The University Press, Cambridge, 1952.

25. WEAVER, A. T. 'Experimental Studies in Vocal Expression.' *J. appl. Psychol.*, 8, 1924, 159–86.

26. WISEMAN, S. 'The Marking of English Composition in Grammar School Selection.' *Brit. J. educ. Psychol.*, 19, 1949, 200–209.

27. WOLTERS, A. W. P. *The Evidence of Our Senses*. Methuen, London, 1933.

28. WOODWORTH, R. S. and SCHLOSBERG, H. *Experimental Psychology*. Methuen, London, 1955.

29. YOUNG, J. Z. 'The Influence of Language on Medicine.' Ch. V in *Studies in Communication*, Vol. I, ed. Evans, I., Secker and Warburg, London, 1955.

CHAPTER 6   *Designing a Test*

The test in spoken English must be a test of achievement, a test to show the standard a pupil has reached at an intermediate point, or at the end, of his school career. It must also be a test which will show him clearly what are his strong and what are his weak points in oral English. (This means that a test at an intermediate point in his school career is really likely to be more valuable than a test at the end, since he will still have time at school in which his weakness can be dealt with.)

We have seen that we need a test of articulacy. We need also a test of the candidate's ability to handle the language of others competently and elegantly – the language of poets or playwrights or story-tellers or scientists. These two elements will make for variety and provide a proper balance. Together they will test a candidate's ability to communicate ideas and feelings to listeners.

Four items which seem to meet these requirements are: (1) The reading aloud of a prose passage or contrasted passages. (2) The speaking of a poem or short passage of poetry. (3) The giving of a talk. (4) A conversation with the examiner.* There are good educa-

* A better name for this test-item would be discussion. 'Conversation' might perhaps suggest the desultory talk that two people, casually meeting for the first time, might have – about the weather, their journeys that morning, a newspaper headline. By Conversation in the context of examining spoken English is meant purposive, directed discussion in which the assessor draws out the candidate, persuading him to talk in such a way that he displays those aspects of speaking which the assessor wishes to examine and judge, notably his linguistic ability. The term conversation is now so widely used by test authorities as the name of a test-item that it seems best to retain it.

tional reasons why other items such as group discussion between two or more candidates, story-telling, improvisation, the acting of short dramatic passages, should be included. It must be remembered, however, that for various reasons an individual test should be short – between ten and fifteen minutes. The four items suggested here have been rigorously tested in experiment; the others have not so far been tested.

The tests now available to schools* are of two kinds, one of which may be called 'private' the other 'public'. In the former the test is a private affair between examiner and examined. (In the experimental stage of one particular test observers were present, but since the tests have been established they are excluded; in another test trainee-assessors sit in with experienced judges to learn the trade.) In the latter there is an audience, usually the classmates of the candidate and interested teachers.

The most important 'private' tests available are those of:

1. The Joint Matriculation Board. An optional test in spoken English is attached to the Board's General Studies papers at 'A Level'. The test consists of two parts: (i) Reading. Candidates are required to read aloud a prose passage or passages which they have had a few minutes to study. (ii) Conversation with the examiner. This may be partly based on the passage(s) used for the test in reading.

2. The University of London School Examinations Council. An optional test in spoken English is attached to the Council's English Language papers at 'O Level'. This consists of two parts, a candidate being required to read aloud a short passage supplied by the examiner and then to converse on simple topics, including questions on the passage read. Both tests aim at assessing the candidate's power of articulation and fluency rather than mere pronunciation. Each candidate is tested for about ten minutes. Candidates are not penalized

---

* 'Available' in the sense that they are provided by external agencies and are available to the schools in certain areas and/or at certain levels of difficulty. There is no reason why schools should not design their own internal tests or why a group of schools in an area should not organize and conduct its own group tests.

for any local dialect or intonation provided that it does not interfere with their ability ˢuccessfully and intelligently to communicate their thoughts to the examiner. Entry is limited to school candidates. A candidate who is successful in the written paper but unsuccessful in the oral test during the summer examination is permitted to take the oral test without having to take the written papers in the following January examination.*

3. The Associated Board of the Royal Schools of Music. Candidates must be prepared: (i) To speak without notes for not less than three or more than five minutes on one subject from a list of six provided by the examiner. Five minutes allowed for the selection of the subject and the preparation of the speech, which is to be done in the examination-room. (ii) To read aloud a passage of prose provided by the examiner. One minute allowed for preparation. (iii) To take part in a short conversation with the examiner on subjects of common interest.

4. The Guildhall School of Music and Drama: Examinations in Spoken English and Public Speaking. There are six grades, the first three, in Spoken English, being suitable for candidates aged 12 to 16. The remaining three are in Spoken English and Public Speaking.

The pattern of the examination for the first three grades is as follows: The candidates will be required (a) to give a prepared talk of not more than five minutes on any one of three named subjects *or* on any other subject of the candidate's choice; (b) *either* to speak from memory any poem from the appropriate graded section of the current G.S.M. and D. Anthology *or* to read a passage chosen by the examiner from a set book or books; (c) to discuss with the examiner a topic from a broad (named) subject appropriate to the

* Until 1964 the University of Durham School Examination Board conducted a test in the Oral Use of English (a 'private' test in the sense used in this chapter). It awarded to successful candidates a Certificate of Proficiency in the Oral Use of English which was in no way connected with the General Certificate Examination. It was intended for Sixth Form candidates and those contemplating entry into a training college in the autumn following the examination, and consisted of the reading aloud of a short prepared prose passage and a conversation with the examiner. The Board was dissolved after the 1964 examinations.

grade (e.g. the highest of the three grades – any subject related to art, theatre, music or literature) and to answer questions on the candidate's speaking and reading.

In the fourth grade, Spoken English and Public Speaking (for which no one under 15 may enter), the candidate is required (a) to deliver a prepared speech of not more than seven minutes on a subject of the candidate's choice; (b) to deliver a prepared speech of not more than four minutes in appreciation of a retiring officer of any organization; (c) to read at sight a passage of prose chosen by the examiner; (d) to discuss with the examiner any points arising from the above, and to answer questions on votes of thanks and interviewing.

In all grades candidates should pay special attention to poise, vocabulary and fluency, clarity of speech and thought, together with a sense of communication. Notes may be used for reference in the presentation of a talk or speech. All talks or speeches should be aimed at specific audiences which should be made known to the examiner.

The most important 'public' test is that of the English Speaking Board whose regulations require the candidate: (1) To speak from memory a passage of verse or prose from the Board's list. (2) To give a prepared talk, render a short dramatic extract or speak a passage of verse or prose of his own choice. (3) To deliver a passage of prepared reading from a book chosen from a list provided by the Board or from the school's English (or any other subject) syllabus. Candidates must bring the prepared reading-book to the examination-room for the examiner to choose any passage. (4) To give a short, impromptu talk. If a 'talk' has been chosen for (2) above this part of the test may be questions and discussion arising from it in which the audience may participate. If drama or a poem has been chosen for (2) the examiner will discover and suggest a subject on which the candidate should be able to give a short exposition. The examination takes place before an audience which may consist of the candidates' classmates and perhaps a few teachers or other interested persons.

These are the well-established tests. In addition to these, tests in oral English are to be part of the examinations in English of the new Regional Boards for the Certificate of Secondary Education, some of which commence in 1965, others in 1966. In all cases where the Boards have so far issued syllabuses (eight, by February 1965) English is to be considered as a single subject, Spoken English carrying 20 per cent of the total mark in five regions and 30 per cent in another.

The tests of three of these Boards consist of Prose Reading and Conversation. The fourth offers a test of Prose Reading and Conversation alternative to a test of Reading and a prepared talk to be followed by question and answer. The fifth provides for Conversation and advises that, in addition, 'the test might well include discussion and debates, dramatic work, short lectures, sensible answering of questions, reading aloud of prose and verse'. The test of the sixth comprises Reading, Conversation and Comprehension; that of the seventh 'Group discussion with an external examiner'. The eighth authority offers two forms of examination: (a) Reading, a four-minute talk with question and answer, and Conversation, all in a group situation; (b) a choice of any two out of nine named activities.

Four of the eight authorities state that the school's estimate of a candidate's ability in spoken English will be considered along with the examiner's estimate.

In order that the wide variety of forms of testing to be made available by the new authorities shall be appreciated the regulations of four of the authorities are set out in full in Appendix 5.

It will be seen that the items of examination common to nearly all tests, 'private' and 'public', are: (a) the reading aloud of prose, and (b) conversation with the examiner. Of the authorities mentioned only the Guildhall School of Music and Drama, the English Speaking Board and the South-Western Examinations Board include the speaking of poetry as a test-item. It is, however, a well-established item in the tests for training-college students of the Institutes of Education of the Universities of Durham and Nottingham, and it is just as 'reliable' (statistically speaking) as the prose reading item of a test.

A little thought will show that of the four items suggested at the beginning of this chapter as being suitable constituents of a test in spoken English conversation is best fitted to the 'private' type of test, the giving of a talk (or the making of a speech) to the 'public' type and prose reading and poetry speaking* are suited to either.

Thus tests can be designed of two or more items: Private – prose reading, verse speaking, conversation; Public – prose reading, verse speaking, the giving of a talk. Each test will last from ten to fifteen minutes (two or three items), including the necessary briefing of the candidate, the change-over from one candidate to the next, and the greeting and farewell.

If the test result is to be used as a record, either within a school as a statement of progress, or externally as a declaration of achievement inscribed on an official document awarded by a reputable examining body; if it is to be helpful to teacher and candidate by revealing the latter's strengths and weaknesses in oral English; and if at the same time it is to have a wide appeal in secondary schools, then certain basic conditions of examination must be observed:

1. The test must be a test of achievement – the achievement of a level of spoken English reached as a result of training in the mother tongue.

2. The test should give the candidate the best opportunity possible to display those aspects of spoken English we wish to rate.

3. It should be so constructed that the speaking performance can be rated easily.

4. The test for each candidate should not take too long (not longer than, say, fifteen minutes). There should, however, be enough time available for the assessor to make, in addition to his ratings, a brief descriptive statement of the strengths and weaknesses of each candidate.

5. Administration should be cheap and easy.

6. The standard of pass should be seen by teachers and children to

* The terms poetry speaking and verse speaking will be used interchangeably throughout this book.

be attainable with reasonable effort (but there must be no suggestion of a 'soft option').

7. The candidate should find the test interesting to take and the immediate preparation stimulating and enjoyable.

8. The test should be both valid and reliable.

Unless a test is both valid and reliable it is worthless. Test authorities are agreed that the leading characteristics of all good measuring instruments are *validity* and *reliability*, although they disagree as to which is the more important. Validity pertains to the truth of the ratings. It refers to the constancy of the functional relation between the scores and the abilities specified by the function; a constant relation means that for any change in score from pupil to pupil there is a corresponding change in the abilities specified.[14] Briefly, we can say that a test is valid if it measures what it purports to measure. Douglas reminds us that a test may be quite valid for measuring one thing and worthless for measuring another; a test is never just valid, it must be valid for *some particular thing*. What are we actually measuring – just what is determining the scores, judgements, or observations we are getting; are we measuring what we suppose we are? If so, how exactly or fully are we measuring it?[7] Validity is easy to define but very difficult to establish and prove either psychologically or statistically. How can we be sure that when we measure a speaking performance or an aspect of it – 'marking' is 'measuring' – we are really measuring what we think we are measuring? There are two main types of evidence bearing on the validity of a test, internal and external. 'Internal' validity is concerned with the content and structure of the test. Do these appear to be reasonable and satisfactory? We 'size up' a test, noting its characteristics, and form a judgement concerning its validity. If we are building a test we take great care in choosing and tailoring the material, in constructing the test and in devising rules for its application. 'External' validity is expressed by the correlation of a test with a criterion, usually other valid and reliable tests in the same field. This is not possible with tests in spoken English, for which the obvious, indeed the only, criterion measure is teachers' marks or ratings. To probe the validity of a test an experimenter must correlate the marks or ratings awarded by a competent external examiner (who has never seen the pupils before and has no record of their abilities or achievements) to a group of pupils, randomly selected, as the result of a test given under standardized conditions, with the marks or ratings awarded to the same group by the teachers who have known and taught them, and have over a long period of time built up a carefully considered speech assessment for each pupil. The comparison of scores with teachers' marks or ratings as a method of determining the degree of validity of a test is based upon two assumptions: (1) that the teachers' marks are measures of the same ability that the test measures;* and (2) that the marks are more accurate indices of the ability than the scores yielded by the test. Making these assumptions, the writer undertook a series of experimental investigations in six schools and six training colleges, probing the validity and reliability of tests in prose reading, conversation, poetry speaking and the giving of a talk (the making of a speech). The results showed that tests in these items of speaking, when conducted by competent examiners under properly organized conditions, have a reasonable validity, measured by correlation coefficients of between $+0.7$ and $+0.8$ (r_t). These figures can be explained in this way. If we have a candidate-list of 100 in a spoken English test conducted by a competent examiner under properly organized conditions and we regard the top 75 per cent as passing and the lower 25 per cent as failing (a possible state of affairs), then we can say that there is a probability that on the average 9 candidates who would be forecast as passing the test by the college or school would be failed by the examiner and 9 who would be forecast to fail would be passed by the examiner, a total misclassification of 18 per cent.†

* An American experimenter, Weaver, in recording his experimental studies in vocal expression, says, 'It is patent that the worth of any test or battery of tests depends upon the character of the criterion with which they are correlated. Unless the criterion actually represents the ability or the aptitude, statistical computation is but vanity.'[25]

† These figures happen to be the same as those quoted for 'reliability'. For a fuller explanation see pp. 30–31.

It is interesting to compare these figures with those for the validity of school examinations of the written essay-type. Professor Valentine has stated that between the orders of a class of, say, 30 boys as recorded in the results of the English and History papers in the old School Certificate examinations and the order of merit drawn up by the teacher of the same class, r equals about + 0·65 on the average of many schools.[22] It seems that tests in spoken English are at least as valid as that type of test in written English most nearly akin, the written essay-type.

The other important characteristic of a good measuring instrument is *reliability*. Two American educational statisticians, Thorndike and Hagen, say that when they ask of a measurement procedure, how reliable is it?, 'We are now asking not what it measures but how accurately it measures whatever it does measure. What is the precision of our resulting score? How accurately will it be reproduced if we measure the individual again? . . . A measure is reliable to the extent that an individual remains nearly the same in repeated measurement – nearly the same as represented by . . . a high reliability coefficient.'[20] The reliability coefficient of a test is an estimate of how much test results may vary if we repeat the testing. It was noted in Chapter 4 that research has shown that the reliability coefficient of a test in spoken English covering the items Prose Reading, Conversation, Poetry Speaking and the giving of a Talk is reckoned to be about + 0·75, representing a probable misclassification of 18 per cent of the candidates when assessed on separate occasions first by one competent assessor, then by a second. It was noted also that this shows spoken English tests to be just about as reliable as written English tests of the essay-type.

A test in spoken English cannot be concerned with *objective* measurement, in which the test itself is the major factor and which can be carried out by any responsible and intelligent person. When we speak of the reliability of a test in which objective measurement is concerned there is no difficulty in our use of the term 'test reliability'. In our tests in spoken English, however, we are dealing with *subjective* measurement, i.e. measurement by impression, in which there are two major factors, the test and the tester. (The candidate is, of course, also an important factor in subjective measurement, liable to fluctuations of behaviour in performance; but he is not a part of the measuring instrument, he is what is being measured.) The tester is not simply a watcher of a machine; he becomes one whole with the instrument he is using. By 'test reliability' in connection with spoken English tests we mean reliability of gradings or ratings made by competent assessors adequately briefed to administer a properly constructed test. We are dealing with the degree of consistency of agreement between assessors. In fact some English educationists prefer to use the term 'consistency' rather than 'reliability'. Professor Valentine speaks of the *consistency of a test*;* Professor Wiseman of the *consistency of the markers*.[28]

The reliability and validity of ratings increase with the number of judges. American experience has shown that the greater the number of judges the higher the reliability of the pooled judgement (based on the mean of scores or ranks). If we can afford more than one assessor for a test in spoken English so much the better.†

CONSTRUCTION OF THE TEST

The Test Items

It is suggested that the basis of a 'private' test for schools (that is to say, one in which there is no audience apart from the examiner) should be prose reading and conversation. These two items are found in nearly all tests available to schools. If they are properly linked these two items form a good basic test for schools, allowing

* 'The consistency of a test is naturally measured by the extent to which a repetition of the test gives the same results. This can be indicated by a correlation coefficient between the two sets of results. Unfortunately, it has become customary for this to be called the reliability coefficient.'[22] Repetition in the case of ratings means repetition of a test producing ratings obtained from additional comparable judges.[8]

† If two or more assessors are employed it is essential to take the average of their several judgements, *made in isolation* (i.e. without discussion). This is what is meant in this book by 'pooled judgements'. If each candidate is discussed various unintended weightings may be embodied in the mark(s) awarded. The most influential assessor may, for example, distort the judgements of his colleagues.

a competent assessor to form an adequate judgement of a candidate's ability in spoken English in a reasonably short space of time – ten minutes. These are very different speaking activities, sharply contrasted. In one the candidate is required to communicate to his auditor as well as he can the meaning and mood of a prose passage or passages, and he has time in which to consider how he can best do this. He can, as it were, take up a prepared position. In the other, as in a boxing match, he has to improvise on the spur of the moment. No preparation of a position is possible – he has to take what comes and make the best of his opportunities. In a sense the assessor is in a position of temporary superiority. He leads the discussion, selects the topics, sets the 'tone'. The candidate must cope not only with words, but also with a person. To the assessor, too, the two activities present strong points of difference. In judging, say, voice or articulation in Prose Reading the assessor can sit back and take a long, cool look at the performance. He is involved, of course, in the total situation, but only incidentally, as the assessor present by virtue of his job. In judging conversation he is involved in a much more fundamental way. As Cherry puts it, the observer-communicant forms part, a very essential part, of the phenomenon he is observing and reporting upon – like the linguist who converses with a native – so that his beliefs and judgements reflect back upon and affect the linguistic behaviour of the partner he observes, and with whom he communicates.[6] He cannot stand outside the situation. He has to take part in the conversation, to support it, to meet the candidate face-to-face and eye-to-eye, and to make his full contribution to the joint performance. An American psychologist, Symonds, has pointed out a difficulty in this situation; there is a possible lack of flexibility in that the mental processes of another person are often intricate and intractable and attain a certain momentum, making it difficult to hold the conversation to the main topic.[19] Such a short time can be made available for any one conversation (say, not more than five minutes) that in this situation the assessor has need of all his patience, powers of understanding, and skill in handling people. He must use his position as the superior in the encounter to guide and control the conversation, making sure as far as he can that the candidate displays, and has the best possible chance to display, those aspects of speaking that he wishes to test. It follows that he cannot, as he can with the other item, Prose Reading, give his whole time to the consideration of the candidate's voice, articulation and whatever other 'details' or aspects he may be required to assess. (One might expect that the 'details' of Prose Reading would be more reliably judged than those of Conversation – especially as assessments of the latter cannot, in the nature of things, be written down as a rule until the *end* of the conversation. In fact, British research suggests that the General Impression mark for Prose Reading (awarded to any candidate by any one of a number of competent raters) is likely to be slightly nearer (on a scale, 0–10) to the average of the group's General Impression Prose Reading marks than the General Impression mark for Conversation (awarded to any candidate by any one of a number of competent raters) is to the average of the group's General Impression Conversation marks. What one might expect is probably the case – Prose Reading tends to be judged rather more consistently than Conversation.

On the other hand there is one important advantage attaching to the judgement of conversation. In prose reading the candidate has a preliminary period of time in which to consider the reading passage or passages, and is therefore able in the test to concentrate on their presentation. The production of voice, the quality of articulation used, can be much more readily controlled than in conversation, in which the candidate must concentrate on content at the expense of the externals of vocal expression. One of the values of conversation as a test is that it enables the examiner to observe the voice and speech of the candidate in a much more natural situation. Both voice and articulation are more likely to resemble the everyday voice and articulation of the candidate.

The 'private' test can be extended to include (prepared) Poetry Speaking, and to it may be added the 'public' giving of a talk. Either would extend the time necessary to fifteen minutes; both to twenty. It would be a great pity to exclude the *giving of a talk* from the options available to the candidates taking a 'private' test. The giving of a talk or the making of a speech is a practical utilitarian exercise which may be of immense personal value to the pupil. (In the opinion of the writer of greater real value to the pupil than the practice of prose reading. Reading aloud, when the attempt is made to do it well – and especially under expert guidance – has valuable indirect results; but the occasions on which in after life a speaker will have cause actually to read to an audience can be few. The practice of speech-making to an audience can have valuable direct results; the ability to speak well in public is an asset that may be put to good use on many occasions in adult life.) Training in this spoken English activity forms a large part of any American course in speech education, whether in school or college; and in universities a very large part of American research in the testing of oral English has dealt with this subject. The giving of a talk is admirably suited to the 'public' test in spoken English (taking place before a group of peers) but as an item in a 'private' test it suffers from one drawback – the speech-making situation provides no real live audience (except the single assessor present) and is felt to be an artificial one. It is therefore suggested that if schools should wish to include the giving of a talk they should make this item a 'public' one and somehow provide an audience for the speaker (perhaps the remainder of the group which is to undergo this item of testing). There is no reason, except the practical one of organization, why 'private' and 'public' items should not be included in one testing programme. On the ground of convenience of organization and because children may be wearied by a twenty-minute test it may be necessary to judge individual items on separate occasions. This may be easy when the spoken English test is an internal one organized and judged by members of a school's teaching staff, but more difficult when the school employs an external examiner.

Schools may have divergent views about the inclusion of a test of Verse Speaking. Many, no doubt, would wish their candidates to take a test which would enable them to show their ability to handle language artistically. Indeed the extremely valuable work done in schools in the artistic speaking of verse is given a keen edge by the prospect of a test and a level of attainment to be recorded. The test is a powerful motivating force. On the other hand many schools may feel that it is unreasonable to compel all those who wish to take a test in spoken English to undergo a test in verse speaking. The speaking of poetry has not the immediately practical value which the command of language offers; and, in any case, some children may have no liking for it and little ability. It seems best that verse speaking should be an optional element in a test.

Verse speaking adds a pleasant touch of variety to the test for pupil and assessor, but its inclusion presents difficulties to both. For the pupil a twenty-minute test that includes the four items of Prose Reading, Verse Speaking, the giving of a Talk and Conversation is a searching one that entails rapid switching of mind and feeling in the sudden consideration of new ideas and new material. (We have noted the possibility of judging the individual items on separate occasions.) It is necessary to provide a short period of rest and silence between one item and the next. This is particularly necessary in the case of Verse Speaking, for the candidate has to be allowed time to soak himself in his verse and recreate the aesthetic apprehension that moved him in the period of preparation. For the assessor the experience is no less exacting. He is asked to 'apprehend aesthetically' at the same time, more or less, as he is assessing under several heads – or, at any rate, to undergo the aesthetic experience in the knowledge that immediately it is over he must make a series of judgements. Sensations will follow thick and fast for him throughout a day's assessing – through the media of prose, poetry, the giving of a talk and the personal impact of successive candidates – and one may wonder when he comes at the end of the day to his fifteenth or eighteenth candidate whether he has any powers of aesthetic apprehension left.

It is suggested that the basis of a 'public' test for schools (that is to say, one in which there is an audience of classmates with, perhaps, some teachers or parents) should be Prose Reading and the giving of a Talk. The latter is a realistic natural activity in such a situation; conversation with the examiner is not. Poetry speaking may be added to make a fifteen-minute test.

. . . . .

F

It appears then that suitable tests can be built up in the following ways:

1. A basic 'private' test (about ten minutes): Prose Reading, Conversation. With a third item (about fifteen) and a fourth (about twenty): either or both, Verse Speaking, the giving of a Talk (the latter being of the 'public' type of test).

2. A basic 'public' test (about ten minutes): Prose Reading, the giving of a Talk. With a third item, Poetry Speaking (fifteen).

These tests are well balanced and likely to prove interesting to both candidates and assessors. The *order* of items in this test is of great importance. Prose Reading and Verse Speaking should come first because rapport has to be established as soon as possible. Candidates are likely to be much more at ease in the difficult early period of the test with those items in which speaking material is provided rather than with those in which the material has to be of their own invention. In a 'public' test the Talk should come last, in a 'private' test the Conversation. In a 'private' test to which has been added the Talk as a 'public' element it would probably be better for various reasons to examine this on a separate occasion. However, if it should be convenient to take all four items in succession the Talk should come third. The Conversation should take place last of all because (a) it is better to prevent the coincidence of the worse phase of a candidate's nervousness with that part of the test in which his speaking material is entirely unprepared, (b) fatigue for the candidate and the assessor is more trying in this item than in any of the other items, and (c) the material for discussion is to be found in the preceding Talk, if there is one; if there is not the initial impetus for Conversation will come from the material or from the style of delivery of the Prose or Verse.

MARKING THE ASPECTS (OR DETAILS) OF THE PERFORMANCE

We now have to ask ourselves a most important series of questions about our testing of spoken English. What is it that the assessor has to look for in his judging? What quality or qualities of a candidate's speaking will he mark as good, what defects as bad? What aspects or details can be reliably judged, and how many of these can be assessed comfortably within a fairly tight schedule, bearing in mind that a set of aspects or 'details' should cover as much as possible of the item to be judged? Is it possible to make a reliable single judgement of the speaking performance (i.e. of the item Prose Reading or Conversation, for example), a 'general impression' of the performance as a whole, represented by a single mark?

Let us consider the last question first. For many years there has been serious discussion, pointed up by a great deal of experimental research, of the marking of written English composition. Two systems of marking have been widely considered – 'general impression' and 'analytic'. In the former a single mark is awarded as the result of an impression judgement, in the latter various elements in the writing are considered (e.g. spelling; punctuation; grammar; range, correctness and appropriateness of information and vocabulary; arrangement and shape; structure of sentences; quantity, quality and control of ideas; paragraphing; sense; power of expression; creative writing) and a sum of 'detail' marks produced. (One experimenter, Cast, reported that examiners appear to fall into two overlapping types: (1) those who mark better by analytic methods, and (2) those who mark better by intuitive or impressionistic methods.)[5] These are the two systems we must consider in the marking of oral English.

In American experimentation each has its own champions. Douglas, an expert in speech-testing, says that speech measurement 'must respond primarily to the total performance or total effect as a unit. Nowhere is the Gestalt principle more demonstrable than in speech behaviour: the whole does not equal the sum of the parts. Adding up scores on individual items to arrive at a sum is a meaningless procedure, especially since we are not able to weigh the individual items with any sound knowledge of the amount they contribute to the whole'.[7] Knower earlier tried to deal with the objection that it is improper to attempt the fragmentation of the speaking situation. He wrote, 'There are some who say that any attempt to break up the speech situation into elements* will ignore the relationship of the elements which is, in many cases, the more

* The aspects or 'details' may be thought of as elements.

important factor. This may sometimes be the case. Like many other educational devices the Rating Scale must be used with judgement.' He quotes Thorndike who said in regard to this criticism of Rating Scales that 'sufficient insight and investigation should enable us to secure all the advantages of the impressionistic judgement* – except its speed and convenience – without any of its defects.' 'Most certainly,' says Knower, 'no one should attempt to use a Rating Scale who has not thoroughly familiarized himself with its contents and method. When this is done it is our experience that, instead of calling attention away from the speaker, it leads to a more strict attention and careful analysis, and increases the interest in critical procedure.'[10] The analytic method has one further advantage over the single General Impression marking – it is much more valuable pedagogically. A test should not only be a record of achievement; it should be a positive help to the candidate who has taken the test and to his teachers by indicating clearly where he is weak and where he is strong. Only the analytic method of marking can do this.

The writer is strongly drawn to the Gestaltists' view that what we see and hear is seen and heard as a 'whole'. (It must not be forgotten that in the face-to-face spoken English test the assessor both sees and hears the candidate and cannot be indifferent to the situation as a whole. We have already noted the interrelation of the senses in this total situation.) While some speech experts may have trained themselves into making 'analytic' judgements (i.e. by abstracting various elements in the speech situation, e.g. voice or verbal ability) and may come to find this the most congenial method of assessment many find it easier to make a 'general impression' judgement, and it is certain that the layman almost always reacts naturally to the speech situation as a whole.

We have so far two methods of scoring. One is to award a General Impression mark for each item, Prose Reading, Poetry Speaking, the giving of a Talk and Conversation. The other is to use an 'analytic' system of marking, abstracting one 'detail' after another from a speaking performance, awarding a mark for it and totalling

* i.e. the advantages of the 'general impression' of the item of the speaking performance to be judged.

72

the series of marks resulting.* Thus a total score for each item (Prose Reading, Conversation, etc.) can be built up by the assessment of a series of 'details', voice, articulation, and one or two others covering the assessment of the candidate's own verbal ability or his ability to interpret the language of others, with subsequent summing of these separate 'detail' scores. There are objections to both methods. A General Impression judgement made by itself is likely to be very woolly and vague and to embody judgements (not made at the level of consciousness) of many aspects of speaking. It has also the pedagogic disadvantage of not indicating to the candidate what are his strengths and weaknesses in his spoken English. A 'Sum of Details' mark ignores the nature of the Gestalt and involves administrative difficulties both for assessor and test authority. The writer suggests that there is a better method of assessment, one which is a combination of the 'general impression' and the 'analytic', and which is free from the strong objections just made to both. Research has shown that if an overall picture of an item of a speaking performance (e.g. Prose Reading or Conversation) has been gradually built up in the mind of the assessor by the process of judging certain individual 'details' in turn, then a final 'general impression' judgement (made quite separately and not by adding and averaging the other 'details') is a stable and reliable one. For the whole test a sum of General Impression marks made in this way is as reliable as a sum of all 'Detail' marks (i.e. a sum of marks awarded for such aspects as voice, articulation, etc.). It is suggested that there should be awarded for each item (Prose Reading, Conversation, etc.) a final single General Impression mark reached in the way described. This mark is specially valuable because it has been steadily built up in the mind of the assessor as he has been rating the individual 'details'. As we have seen the practical value of this is that, if marking has been done in this way, a set of General Impression marks submitted to an examining authority is likely to prove just as reliable a set of scores

---

* It must be noted that this system of marking is simply another form of marking by impression. Instead of considering the whole the assessor narrows his field and considers one small part of the whole after another, marking each by subjective impression.

as a 'Sum of Details', and it is much less cumbersome for assessor and examining authority. There is still the pedagogic objection that the single General Impression mark for each item fails to indicate to the candidate his strong and weak points. The writer, in his training-college marking of these and other items, builds up his single General Impression by the method discussed, and from the 'detail' marking (and from running notes he has made on a separate sheet of paper) is able to add to this mark a brief descriptive statement of the strengths and weaknesses of each candidate's performance. It is suggested that this can be done for the school tests proposed in this book.

We will leave aside for the moment the consideration of what 'details' should be judged before a General Impression is assessed. When this assessment is made these 'details' receive considerable weight. The General Impression will, however, be the impression of a natural whole, and will not exclude 'the dynamic and static aspects of posture and movement including the whole range of phenomena relating to the bodily manifestation of a person and of facial expression'.[15] The General Impression of Speech-making (or, as we may call it for schools, the giving of a Talk) may take into consideration all these things together with a vague estimate of the speaker's friendliness, good humour, sincerity, and his success in choosing and organizing his material according to a logical plan that will produce a complete speech or talk within the time allowed. To judge the performance as a whole will almost certainly bring into consideration (albeit not on the surface of consciousness) these and other elements of presentation, some of which, like *pronunciation*, are common to all assessors, and others which come into play in the judgement of some assessors and not in those of others.

We now come to the choosing of the preliminary 'details', a matter of the utmost importance, since these will enter largely into the formation of the General Impression judgement, and will form the standardizing element as between assessor and assessor (and thus become the basis of the reliability of the General Impression judgement).

These 'details' should 'overlap' as little as possible, and it should be possible to describe them fairly exactly – at least at either end of a continuum representing very good and very poor, so that with proper briefing assessors will have a good idea of what it is they are supposed to be judging.

It is a commonplace of testing (especially in America where much more speech-testing is done than in England) to require examiners to judge candidates in speech-making (or those giving a talk) both as to delivery and content. Lantz considered the problem of whether listeners to a speech who were instructed to concentrate on both content and delivery perceived content as efficiently as listeners instructed to concentrate on content, and whether they perceived delivery as efficiently as listeners instructed to concentrate on delivery. His experimental results suggested that concentration on both factors could give as great perception of each as concentration on each one alone.[12] As the result of recent experimentation in the University of Iowa, Becker came to the conclusion that although assessors might be asked to rate a whole range of 'details' in the judging of Speech-making (analysis, material, organization, language, adjustment of speaker, bodily action, voice, articulation and pronunciation, fluency, etc.) they were in fact discriminating only three: an analysis-content factor, a delivery factor and a language factor. It appeared that language was the most independent of the elements; that is to say that, when the assessors were rating the 'detail' language, their judgements were not getting mixed up with those they were making about either of the other two factors.[4]

Thus, possible 'details' for the giving of a Talk seem of three sorts, each of which should be represented, if only by one 'detail', in a test in spoken English: (a) those covering the manner of speaking, (b) those covering the candidate's ability to use language, (c) those covering the organization and content of his speech. Possible 'details' for the Conversation item of a test are of the two sorts, (a) delivery aspects, (b) language aspects. (It does not seem reasonable or practical to use (c) above for Conversation.) We can, in choosing 'details' for these three factor-categories, largely avoid overlap.

In the sorts of 'details' that may be chosen to give a balanced view of the two 'items', Prose Reading and Verse Speaking, it does not seem possible to achieve such a sharp distinction. The candidate is interpreter; his appreciation or understanding of content is reflected in his style of delivery in the act of interpretation and communication.

In American research into the reliability of judgements of various forms of speaking, including speech-making, two of the elements of presentation freely used are *voice* and *articulation*. In published Rating Scales (for use in American schools and colleges) these two elements are included for contribution to a total score. The American Council on Education's pre-war 'Personality Measurement Scale' included *voice* and *distinctiveness of articulation* as two of the elements to be rated.[2] Sometimes there is a section to be rated called 'vocal expression' with sub-elements, projection, general pitch level, flexibility, quality (all aspects of voice in action). Two of the basic speech proficiency requirements of the member institutions of the American Association of Colleges for Teacher Education are (a) articulation and enunciation, (b) agreeable voice quality, and the two most generally tested elements of speaking in American educational institutions are *articulation-enunciation* and *voice*. The writer has also used voice and articulation in his 'running judgements' of Prose Reading, Poetry Speaking, Speech-Making and Conversation as aids to a final single recorded judgement.

Voice is sound produced primarily by the vibration of the vocal bands. The term 'quality', when applied to voice, is used of the acoustic characteristics of vowels resulting from their overtone structure or the relative intensities of their frequency components.[29] It is sometimes called 'timbre' or 'vocal colour' and is the characteristic by which we distinguish between two voices uttering the same vowel at the same pitch, or between two different vowels uttered by the same voice at the same pitch. It is also the characteristic by which we distinguish generally between two voices. The 'quality' is a subjective experience dependent partly upon other factors than overtone structure, while the latter is a physically measurable aspect of the tone.[26] In more general terms voice is expressive movement, an individual pattern composed of such inextricable factors as pitch, rhythm, intensity, inflection, volume and vocal mannerisms. Voice is, in brief, the external form of vocal expression (speech, on the other hand, being its content).[1]

To define voice, however, is not the same thing as to lay down standards for judging 'good' and 'poor' voice. Voice in speaking is judged in context. When we listen to a person's voice, as in judging, we cannot help being affected by the total presentation of the person; i.e. presence and personality must enter into our apprehension of his voice. The evaluation that results is thus, to some extent, qualified by a 'General Impression'. A speech delivered in a 'corn-crake' voice may be a great success, because the voice exactly fits the personality of the speaker and enables him to produce the maximum effect on his audience. This is an extreme case, but it does emphasize a difficulty for the test designer who must ensure that his choice of material for the test item – prose, poetry, etc. – discourages the use of any method of voice production that is inefficient.*

An American expert suggests that the ideal speaking voice should do the work allotted to it, as does any other efficient mechanism, with a minimum expenditure of energy for a maximum effect and aesthetic gratification. Happily, he says, the achievement of one criterion of efficient voice production implies achievement of them all. The most pleasant voice a person can produce will be achieved only when the vocal strain is minimal and the vocal effect is maximal.[16]

While there is agreement amongst the experts on the definition of *voice*, there is no such agreement on that of *articulation*. The terms *articulation*, *diction*, *enunciation* are variously used to refer loosely to

* This raises a question – should candidates be allowed to choose their own test material? For strict comparison of performances (i.e. for statistical respect-ability) – no. In practice a choice is often allowed by testing authorities in the items, Poetry Speaking and the giving of a Talk, subject to certain necessary safeguards. In any case the statistical objection must be set aside in the case of Conversation, for no two conversations are ever exactly alike. (Cherry says that each individual and each conversation is unique.)[6] If it does not apply here it cannot in reason apply to the other items. The candidate will, in the nature of things, have no choice in the matter of the unseen prose reading material, but often here the assessor will be provided with a number of passages one of which *he* will choose for a candidate. (Variety of material helps to preserve the sanity of the assessor and, indirectly, makes for better testing.)

the movements of the speech organs in and about the mouth in making the sounds of speech. Here there is often confusion between the meanings of these terms and that of pronunciation. Unfortunately there is no definitive glossary of speech terms for the ordinary speech practitioner. Wood regrets the looseness and ambiguity (among people who use them) of the definitions of most of the terms in the field of speech, but points out that it is not the function of a glossary or dictionary to create terms or to assign meanings; these should clarify and reflect, in so far as possible, the usages among the professional members of the field. He defines the term articulation, in speech, as 'the production of individual sounds in connected discourse; the movement and placement during speech of the organs which serve to interrupt or modify the voiced or unvoiced airstream into meaningful sounds; the speech function performed largely through the movements of the lower jaw, lips, tongue and soft palate'.[29]

Two American voice-scientists (Judson and Weaver) define articulation in terms which go some way to answering our question about a possible relationship between articulation and voice. They say, 'Speech sounds, other than the vowels, may be thought of as initiators, connectors or terminators of vowel sounds – i.e. these speech sounds are vowel links. . . . All vowel links owe, as do the vowels, some of their individual peculiar acoustic characteristics to resonance. In addition all vowel links require modifications . . . before each has acquired the entire set of individual characteristics peculiar to itself. These additional modifications we call *articulation*. Articulation, then, is the breaking-up or interruption of the phonated or non-phonated breath-stream, and with the important aid of resonance, the finished products are the vowel-links. Articulation takes place within, or because of, structures in or closely connected with the oral cavity. . . . The vowel links may be classified as consonants, nasals and vowel glides.'[9]

This is the definition the writer suggests should be adopted. In brief, the assessment of articulation should be the assessment of the making of consonants, including the nasals [m, n, ŋ] and the vowel glides [w. j] – i.e. the speech sounds other than the vowels

– in connected discourse (whether in the reading aloud of prose, the speaking of poetry, the making of a speech, or in conversation).

It is obvious that *voice* and *articulation* have central cores of difference. It was suggested earlier that there may also be an 'overlap' in these two elements of presentation and that a judge, when assessing one, may also be taking into account some factor or factors present also in the other. The voice-scientists, Judson and Weaver, have suggested one common factor – resonance.[9] It seems certain that the presence of resonance in voiced consonants contributes to the judge's apprehension of the total voice-quality that he is judging. It seems certain also that the quality of articulation will, to a certain extent, affect the quality of voice. If a speaker has a tight jaw, or if he scarcely opens his mouth when speaking, or if he fails to make the right amount of pressure on labial plosives [p, b], or if he is much addicted to glottal stops, the voice is affected. If he has a flexible jaw, lips and velum and uses an adequate but unobtrusive articulation the quality of voice is likely to be different from those qualities of voice resulting from tight jaw, over-strong or feeble lip-action, etc.

There is a further difficulty, one inherent in the method of subjective judgement. The act of speaking is one of total presentation and it is certain that some assessors find it difficult to abstract one 'detail' while ignoring cues from the others. As one might expect assessors fall into three broad, ill-defined groups, those who can discriminate clearly between 'details', those who cannot discriminate at all (i.e. those who have a 'halo' running through all their judgements), and those who come somewhere roughly between the other two groups. In this matter research evidence concerning voice and articulation is inconclusive. Some schools, when considering the design of a test in spoken English, might well prefer to ask their assessors not to judge voice and articulation separately but to judge a composite 'detail', *voice/articulation*, which could be called *delivery*. As the American practice of separating the 'details' is so well established the writer has included both in his Rating Scale (Appendix 2). It is proposed that these two aspects of the manner of delivery should be included in the series of judgements to be made about each item – Prose Reading, Poetry Speaking, the giving of a Talk, Conversation.*

It has been noted earlier that in the case of prose reading and poetry speaking it seems just as important to judge the candidate's appreciation or understanding of content as of his use of voice and articulation; yet in the act of communication understanding is reflected in style of delivery. Voice and articulation stand for two elements (perhaps partially linked) of presentation. The writer suggests a third 'detail' – *interpretation*, which in this context conveys the idea of dynamic presentation of the candidate's appreciation or understanding of the content of the prose or poetry material. 'Overlap' can be avoided to a large extent by the assessor's concentrating on elements of presentation other than voice and articulation, e.g. phrasing, intonation, pace, pause, stance, gesture. It is idle to pretend that it can be done without overlap, for the voice is an ever-present vehicle of interpretation.

We have seen that for the other two possible items of testing, viz. the giving of a Talk and Conversation, there is a clear distinction to be drawn between two sorts of 'details' to be judged: (a) those covering the manner of speaking, (b) those covering the candidate's ability to handle language. For (a) voice and diction have been suggested. For (b) it is suggested that there could be common to both Conversation and the giving of a Talk a 'detail' to stand for the ability to handle language in the speaking situation – *power of verbal expression*. This 'detail' would cover the ability of the candidate in Conversation and in the Talk to use clear, accurate, varied and vivid language competently structured, both vocabulary and structure being appropriate to the subject and the audience. It would also, for the Conversation 'detail', cover the candidate's ability to state a case, to develop a theme, to rebut an argument, to show some skill

* It is not enough to make judgements of voice and articulation on the evidence of the prose reading test only. We have seen that for the candidate the problems of involvement in prose reading are different from those of involvement in conversation. Under the stress of the conversation test situation the voice and articulation he uses may be somewhat different from those he will produce in the prose reading test situation, over which, as we have seen, he is likely to have more control.

in the imparting of information and the answering of questions, in narration, description and perhaps persuasion.

It has been suggested earlier that for the giving of a talk there should be a detail to be rated covering organization and content. It seems appropriate to call this 'detail' *organization and content*. It would cover the candidate's ability to choose interesting and relevant material of good quality for his talk and to plan and organize it competently, having in mind the audience for which it is intended.

Pronunciation might seem to be an obvious speech element for inclusion in the list of 'details' of a test in spoken English. Yet it presents great difficulties. In the first place there is the same difficulty of definition that we have seen to arise in the matter of articulation/enunciation. Since the writer is going to propose that pronunciation be *not* included as an aspect of a speaking performance about which a separate judgement is to be made, the steps by which he reached the following definition in the context of testing can be omitted: *Pronunciation* is the acoustic effect produced by the making of speech sounds (*all* speech-sounds – vowels, consonants, semi-vowels). Secondly, there is the perhaps insuperable problem of laying down standards. Who is to say what is 'good' pronunciation and what is 'poor'? If we are not to be allowed to say that 'Standard English' is 'better' than Yorkshire or Hampshire pronunciation – and we ought not to be so allowed – then we are left with the impossible task of defining 'good' Yorkshire and 'poor' Yorkshire if we are to judge pronunciation in a Yorkshire school, and 'good' Hampshire and 'poor' Hampshire if we are to judge in a Hampshire school. What we can do with this approach is to say that in *London schools only* we can regard the two ends of the rating continuum of pronunciation as being represented at the 'good' end by the pronunciation of Standard English as recorded in Daniel Jones's Pronouncing Dictionary, and at the 'poor' end by 'broad Cockney', with the varying degrees of Cockney flavour from 'mild' to 'strong' representing the intermediate ranges. We can do this only because philologists now agree that modern 'Standard' English is historically derived (as Cockney is) from the East Midlands dialect of Chaucer's time, a dialect in full living use in his time in the geographical triangle – Cambridge/London/Oxford. If a test authority operating in the London area, or schools in the London area, wish to include pronunciation as a 'detail' to be judged in a spoken English test it thus appears perfectly reasonable to do so. (One must assume, of course, that the children taking the test would be London children.) Indeed, the writer's experience is that assessors find no difficulty in judging this 'detail'. The writer recommends that pronunciation be not included simply because its inclusion makes no difference to the reliability of a spoken English test. It cannot be used as a 'detail' in a test to be held outside the London area, and it is scarcely worth the extra effort the judge must make in a test within it.

However, we cannot pretend that pronunciation as an influence in men's minds does not exist; it is still there as an element in a speaking performance. It will make its effect upon the listener – the assessor – however impartial he may try to be. It is obvious that assessors need guidance in dealing with this element of speaking. In the 'Briefing Instructions' attached to the proposed Rating Scale (Appendix 2) will be found the following:

NOTES: PRONUNCIATION

Assessors should be asked to note:

(a) that pronunciation should not at all affect their judgement of (i) voice or (ii) articulation, except in so far as the making of speech sounds may result in a form of voice-production or articulation, respectively, poorer than that described in the Rating Scale against the marks 9, 10, (iii) interpretation or (iv) power of verbal expression, except in so far as ease of comprehension is affected;

(b) that the General Impression mark should, however, represent an impression and that they should not try to exclude pronunciation.

It will be seen that the 'details' suggested for assessment are:

Prose Reading ⎫ Poetry Speaking ⎬	Voice, diction, interpretation.
The giving of a Talk	Voice, diction, power of verbal expression, organization and content.

Conversation   Voice, diction, power of verbal expression.

For each item   General Impression.

It is stressed once more that the General Impression in each item should be assessed after the marks have been awarded for all the other 'details', and that this assessment should be made without reference to the other 'detail' marks. It should certainly *not* be an average of their total. The General Impression marks are the important assessments: only these should be returned to the examining authority.

THE TEST MATERIAL

It is obvious that test material must be chosen carefully. Its choice will depend upon the answers we give to the questions posed for the test-designer at the beginning of the last section. What is it that the assessor has to look for in his judging? What quality or qualities of a candidate's speaking will he mark as good, what defects as bad? It will be helpful to discuss these questions and the choice of test material in connection with each item of the test.

Prose Reading

If a candidate is standing in front of an audience, reading, what is the paramount consideration in the mind of the assessor? It is surely a consideration of communication. Is the reader reading *to* his audience? Is he aware of them? Is he trying to get in touch with them? Is he interested in the printed material and is he sparking off and sustaining an interest on the part of the audience? Is he helping the audience, as he reads, to recreate for themselves the meaning and mood of the passage?

If he is doing these things then it is clear that he understands the passage. (To read well requires an intelligent appreciation of the meaning and mood of the piece of prose.) He will be presenting his interpretation of the print by means of skilful phrasing, fluent rhythm, expressive intonation, the flexible use of pace and pause. Since a well-produced voice is, generally speaking, the pleasantest to listen to, his breathing will be well-managed (and unobtrusive), his voice well-pitched (subjecting the throat to no strain) and capable of response to changes of atmosphere and mood in the prose passage. His articulation will be crisp but unobtrusive and unaffected. He can be heard easily and he will be easy to listen to. In such circumstances the assessor will wish to give him high marks. The Rating Scale suggested (Appendix 2) sets these points out clearly. It also sets out the reverse of the medal at the other end of the assessment continuum.

On the whole it is considered that two short, sharply contrasted passages of prose reveal the candidate's merits and defects better than one longer one does; but if circumstances suggest that it is better to use only one then a longer passage, carefully chosen, can prove very satisfactory.

This is perhaps a suitable point to touch briefly on the question of the preparation time to be allowed. To ask a candidate to read *entirely* unseen a passage of prose, and to read it well, is to set him a very difficult task. In fact all test authorities allow a candidate at least sufficient time to look through the passage in order to get the gist of it. The Associated Board of the Royal Schools of Music allows a minute. Even so the task is a difficult one. The test becomes somewhat easier (and perhaps allows better opportunity at some levels for the display of those aspects of speaking the examiner wishes to assess) if, as one candidate is being examined in, say, a ten-minute test, the next is looking over the prose passage(s) for reading. This is considered to be 'unprepared' prose reading. (Rightly so; in the case of 'prepared' verse speaking the verse can be prepared days, or even weeks, beforehand.)

Certain principles involved in the choice of material are suggested by the points we have been considering.

(a) The material must be interesting to candidates and audience.

(b) The literary style should not be remote from that of spoken English of the present day.

(c) Each passage should be fairly complete in itself.

(d) It should be chosen with due regard to the age and general intelligence of the pupils for whom it is intended. In any particular examination the alternative passages of test material (if alternatives are used) should be of roughly the same standard of difficulty.

(e) Passages should be long enough to allow the assessor time to examine carefully the details they are seeking to judge (voice, articulation, etc.), say about 150–200 words if two are used and about 300–400 if only one.

(f) There should be either two strongly contrasted short passages in each prose reading item or one longer one.

(g) There should be several sets of passages available for the *assessor's* choice.

(h) It is useful to prepare a few questions on each passage to serve as a lead-in to conversation.

Sample passages, shorter and longer, will be found in Appendix 1. Let us consider three linked pairs of short passages. (Follow-up questions are included in the appendix.)

1. 'An English Conductor' and 'The Octopus'.

The first is a brief anecdote, light and amusing, the point of the story being the impact upon a Hungarian audience made by a catenation of sounds, common enough in English – [sps], but unexpected and amusing to Hungarian ears. The speaker and his hearers are uninvolved. 'The Octopus' describes the attack by an octopus on a feeding crab. The speaker and his hearers are heavily involved, for this is murder. In this short piece there are colour, movement, horror and death.

2. 'The Nature of Scientific Prose' and 'An Incident of the Great Frost: The King's Carnival.'

The first short passage illustrates the nature of scientific prose by quoting a physicist's description of a rainbow – an accurate statement of the principles underlying the formation of the rainbow, but entirely devoid of the sense of beauty and the feeling of wonderment evoked in ordinary men and women. The second passage, a description of the carnival scene on the river at night during the Great Frost at the beginning of the seventeenth century, suggests the sense of beauty and the feeling of wonder – and a disregard of scientific accuracy.

3. 'The Spirit of Science' and 'Memories of Christmas'.

The first extract is factual; the listener is invited to consider some imaginary graphs of the very best man has been able to accomplish along various lines of human achievement at different times in history – travel, the rate of transmission of news, power, craftsman-ship. All our graphs, after running flat for ten thousand years, have suddenly taken a tremendous upward turn and are still going up steeply. The second is an imaginative recall by Dylan Thomas, in a magnificent flurry of powerful adjectives, of a Christmas memory of snow and snowballing, cats and the outbreak of fire.

In each of these cases the passages, which are sharply contrasted, require different styles of oral English, and together they provide material for a good test, at an elementary level, of a candidate's ability to read prose aloud.

It is clear that a candidate must be allowed a brief interval of time between his reading of the first and his reading of the second, time in which to rid himself of the mood and feeling engendered by the first, and to prepare for the mood and feeling that he knows the second will arouse in him, and that he must project to his audience.

Poetry Speaking

Our discussion of the problem of communication in the reading of prose is equally relevant to the speaking of poetry. A poem could be chosen for prepared poetry speaking which might excite the aesthetic apprehension of the candidate and, in his rendering of it, that of the assessor and audience (if there is one). With what quality of imagination, what degree of sensitivity, can the candidate inform his speaking of the poem? A short period of rest and silence (which, it is suggested, should be allowed between one item and the next) is particularly necessary before the speaking of poetry in order to allow the candidate time to soak himself in his passage of verse and recreate the 'aesthetic apprehension' that moved him in the period of preparation.

Certain principles are involved in the choice of material:

(a) It has been suggested earlier that it is not reasonable to ask all candidates in any examination to speak the same poem or the same verse-passage. There are two alternatives:

(i) To allow each candidate to speak a poem of his own choice.

(ii) To allow each candidate to choose a poem from a varied list drawn up by the test authority (i.e. the external testing board or the school authorities).

The first alternative is not really feasible. It is statistically unsound, resulting in any one examination in a wide range of passages of verse of widely differing degrees of difficulty. The remaining alternative (ii) is the one recommended by the writer, with the provision that the test authority should ensure that the poems on its list do not differ greatly in length and are roughly of the same degree of difficulty of presentation.

(b) Further, the selection of poems should be such that to speak them effectively would seem to exclude the use of voice that might be described as 'harsh', 'hoarse', 'strained', or indeed that might be described by any of the epithets used in the Rating Scale for voice at the lower end of the continuum – see Appendix 2. (In the case of some poems, e.g. some of those with a dramatic content, it might reasonably be argued that one could, or should, speak them with a 'hoarse' or 'strained', etc., voice.) J. C. Squire's 'The Discovery' is an example of a poem that seems to satisfy this condition; it is suggested as being suitable at almost any stage in the secondary school. (See Appendix 1.)

(c) The poems should be complete in themselves (i.e. either complete poems or passages of poetry that have a reasonable completeness within the permitted length).

(d) They should be long enough to allow the assessor time to make his judgements. The minimum is sonnet-length.

The Talk or Speech

If our candidate is again standing in front of an audience, this time addressing them in a talk or in a speech, what special quality in the candidate and his speaking is the assessor seeking? It is surely immediacy of communication. A good speaker will interest his audience, whether his talk is to inform, to persuade or simply to entertain. Quite early in the talk he will have established rapport with his audience; they will be in a state of sympathy with him, willing to be informed, instructed or persuaded. He will have won their sympathetic attention and will continue to hold it by his manner of speaking and style of delivery, by the content of his discourse and the way he has planned it, and by his power of verbal expression.

His voice will be free of tensions and well-pitched, his articulation clear but unobtrusive. His style of speaking will be unaffected, direct, sincere; there will be no mannerisms. He will be friendly and good-humoured. His physical presence will be harmoniously expressive in body, hands, face.

His talk will be well-constructed. There will be a good introduction, a middle and a conclusion. His material will be well chosen and well organized to produce a complete talk within the time allowed. He will make his main points clearly, avoiding unnecessary repetition. (A repetition of the main heads of his talk as a final 'clinching' or summing-up may be judged to be useful, even necessary.) He will express his meaning clearly with a spontaneous and fluent command of language. He will exercise a discriminating choice of words from a suitable vocabulary of adequate range.*

One may say that this is to demand too much of schoolchildren; and so it is of all but the few. But these requirements are set down to show the sorts of consideration that should influence the assessor in his making of judgements. The levels of performance required can be adjusted by the test authorities to the groups of candidates to be tested.

* These aspects of delivery and content of the talk must be judged in terms of the audience which the speaker has in mind, which should be, of course, the audience in front of him. It is not fair to ask the candidate to beam his talk at too heterogeneous an audience. It is suggested that the candidate should be asked to talk to his peers (classmates or children in parallel forms). If parents, teachers, educational administrators and others are present they should be regarded merely as observers; in fairness to the candidate there should not be many of these.

It is not reasonable to set in a school examination a single subject and expect all candidates to speak to it. Some choice must be given. The Associated Board of the Royal Schools of Music allows a choice from a list of half a dozen subjects. (The choice is really wider than this suggests. In the current regulations the first subject is: Describe any interesting building, factory, or ship that you have visited.) The half-dozen subjects include description, discussion, narrative and fantasy. The choice is wide and gives the candidate considerable scope, but there are limits to it. Five minutes are allowed for the selection of the subject and the preparation of the speech, which must be done in the examination-room. This test is designed for candidates approaching the Ordinary Level of the General Certificate of Education. Its conditions will obviously make it too difficult for many children.

A much easier form of test is the 'public' type of test of the English Speaking Board. In this case the candidate chooses his own subject and is encouraged to have his talk well prepared before the examination. In any one school examination there is a wide scope of subject matter. An excellent feature of these 'Own Choice' prepared talks is that children are encouraged to use illustrative aids (where they can be aptly applied), such as models, specimens, diagrams, apparatus, etc.

An advantage of this second type of test is that it can be geared to almost any school age-group or streaming-level. It is an excellent test for those taking their first oral examination which includes the talk as an item (or for those afflicted by 'nerves'), since everything can be prepared beforehand. This is also its weakness, for there is no reason why the text of the talk should not be learned by heart. The test for many candidates will not be sufficiently demanding.

There is a third type of test, one which allows a large measure of preparation in the days before the examination, but excludes the possibility of the writing out and learning of the talk or speech at leisure. The candidate chooses three broad topics and prepares plenty of background material for each. He can be said to know each topic-area fairly thoroughly. The assessor is informed of the three topic-areas, selects one of them and offers to the candidate a subject based on this topic-area. Given his 'slant' on the general theme he is required to compose a talk or speech, i.e. to select, shape, put his material in order and develop his subject.

Let us consider what might happen in the case of a bright boy aged 14 or 15. He looks at television regularly but is fairly selective in his viewing. There is much to think of and talk about in this area of interest, so he decides that 'Television' shall be one of his topics. He has been abroad several times, sometimes with his parents, once or twice with a youth organization, and once on a school journey. He has particularly enjoyed camping in France. For his second option he chooses 'Holidays Abroad'. He feels that he has a great deal of information and personal experience on which to draw and that he could interest an audience of his peers. He considers his third topic: what shall it be? He is a keen member of his local youth club. He could make an interesting talk out of the material of his activities and experiences. Certainly he has a great deal of material to hand. However, he has been making a special study at school as a project of his own in his History course – 'The House of Commons'. He has a file (with a picture of the House on the front page) which he has lovingly illustrated with cuttings, pictures and diagrams. It contains several compositions he has already written on various aspects of his subject and a large amount of carefully organized information in the form of notes. His Member of Parliament has shown him and his friends round the House (giving them a nice tea, too) and has talked to them of the vital part it has played and still plays in the life of the nation. This topic he thinks will be his third option. He is now prepared with background material on three topics and comes to the examination-room with notes on all three. Let us suppose that the assessor chooses the boy's third option, 'The House of Commons'. He then *offers* a subject which he hopes the boy may feel able to cope with; say, 'The Party system in the House of Commons: how it works'. If the boy thinks he can organize a talk on this subject he accepts it. If he considers this to be too difficult he will say so. Between them assessor and candidate may decide on 'Mr. Speaker' or 'The House of Commons: what it is and what it does'.* The important point is that both have agreed on a subject for which the candidate has enough material. The assessor must see that for the general standard of this particular examination the subject selected is at the appropriate level of difficulty.

This type of test can be made easier for the candidate by requiring him to present two topic areas instead of three, or only one.

If this third type of test is adopted time for preparation of the subject must be allowed. It is suggested that just before the previous candidate is examined the assessor should talk with the pupil and agree on a subject. In a three-item test there will be enough time during the examination of the previous candidate for the necessary preparation. In a two-item test there may not be. The shortness of the time available (ten minutes for the reading through of the prose passage and the preparation of the talk) can be used as one of the difficulty-variables available to the testing authority. If it is desired to give plenty of time the candidate should be allowed to spread his preparation over the time allotted for the two candidates immediately preceding, i.e. twenty minutes.

It will be seen that if the subjects for the talk or speech set for a test of the first type were of equal difficulty and complexity with those set for tests of the second and third types then the actual test of the first type would be the most difficult of these, that of the third would come next in order of difficulty, and that of the second would be the easiest sort of test. (For example, a talk entitled 'My Favourite Television Programmes' would be easiest for the candidate if he knew the title well in advance of the day of examination and could prepare it at leisure, it would be less easy if he had prepared in advance only the background material on the topic 'Television' and had a quarter of an hour in which to prepare the subject 'My

* The topic 'Television' might have produced subjects such as 'My Favourite Programmes', 'Learning by Television', 'Why I prefer Television to the Cinema'; the topic 'Youth Clubs' such subjects as 'An Evening spent at my Youth Club', 'Youth Clubs; their value to the nation', 'Youth Club Activities'; the topic 'Holidays Abroad' such subjects as 'Camping in France', 'Why I like Switzerland', 'Youth Hostels in Western Europe'.

Favourite Television Programmes', and it would be most difficult for him if he were given this title in the examination-room with five minutes only in which to prepare the talk.) But this order of difficulty of the various types can be modified by making the talk-subject of greater or less complexity. Thus girls might well find it easier to give a talk on 'How to Make an Apple Pie' with little or no preparation than to give a talk prepared at leisure beforehand on 'Careers for Women'.

It is not proposed here to say that one type of the test-item, Talk or Speech, is better than the others; any one of the three types might best fit the circumstances of a particular school.

The following principles should apply to the Talk or Speech item of a test:

(a) The subject of the talk or speech should be of interest to the candidate and to the audience.

(b) No complete speech should be written out and read to the audience, although the candidate should be permitted to have his talk on a sheet or sheets of paper in note form.

(c) From three to five minutes should be allowed for the delivery of the talk or speech.

(d) Candidates should be allowed (and encouraged if it is likely to enhance the value of the talk) to use a blackboard, properties, visual and aural aids; and to have the help of other pupils or students to illustrate their talks.

Conversation

Let us suppose that our assessor and candidate have reached the last item of the 'private' test, Conversation. (It will be remembered that this item has been recommended for the 'private' test only, i.e. that in which nobody is present but candidate and assessor.) The assessor as the dominant partner must now ease the candidate gently into a happy speaker–listener relationship. He must make sure there is no awkward pause in which tension has a chance to build up. A useful way to begin is to make use of simple questions based on the prose passage(s) used in the text.

In Appendix 1 are to be found questions based on the two prose passages described earlier in this chapter. They are of varying difficulty:

1. Which passage do you prefer? (Why?) OR 2. Can you mention one big difference between the two passages? 3. Is there, do you think, any difference between listening to an orchestra on the wireless and listening to it in the concert hall? (What differences?) 4. Is the second passage a *scientific* description of an octopus? (If not, why not?), etc. These questions are suggested primarily as a lead-in to conversation and not as an interrogatory in which question and answer expose the candidate's lack of knowledge. No candidate should be penalized for failing to give a correct answer. It is possible, however, that a satisfactory conversation might develop from one of these questions. If it appears unlikely then one or more of the others can be tried. Failing this the assessor should draw on a list of topics for discussion (carefully compiled beforehand), graded according to the standard of the test. Sample topics are: 1. Newspapers, magazines, books; 2. Favourite subject (possibly leading to discussion of career); 3. School journeys (home and abroad) OR Holidays (camp? overseas? family? etc.); 4. The area from which the school population is drawn (its factories, buildings, civic centre, parks, people, etc.); 5. School sports; 6. Hobbies. The first one (which might be any on the list), deliberately introduced, or led into from the preliminary questions, might prove satisfactory and no others would be needed. However, if one subject failed, the others would be available to try. A skilful and friendly assessor ought soon to be able to light on a subject on which the candidate will talk freely. It must be remembered also that nibbles at too many disparate subjects will not make a good conversation, one essential ingredient of which is continuity.

In the conversation test it is important that there should be plenty of material available to the candidate. If the topics already proposed are thought to be too difficult for a test at a chosen level it is suggested that the single prepared topic be used. In this case the candidate prepares plenty of material for a chosen topic (perhaps with guidance from his class-teacher as to subject and subject-divisions and the collection of material). The assessor, by careful feeding-in of appropriate questions and occasional comment, can keep the candidate talking to some purpose (and ensure that material learned by heart is not 'talked at' him).

As we have already seen the assessor is deeply involved in the conversation. He must use his position as the superior in the encounter to guide and control the conversation, making sure as far as he can that the candidate displays, and has the best chance to display, those aspects of speaking which he wishes to assess. (Watts has reminded us that the extent of a child's power over language will naturally be looked for in his conversation.)[24] Communication is always a two-way process, but this time the assessor plays a much more positive and vital role. He is concerned to note how well the candidate plays his part, but it is his duty to sustain and encourage him. It has been suggested that it is useful to have one or two questions on the prose passage available as a 'lead-in'. While, in the circumstances, it will thus be natural and perhaps necessary to begin the conversation with a question – and keep it moving with an occasional query – the assessor must avoid asking a string of personal questions that may make the interchange a sort of 'third-degree' interrogation. The aim of questioning, once the conversation-topic is under way, should be to ensure to the conversation that vital characteristic without which it can scarcely be called conversation – continuity.

The good candidate will successfully maintain in conversation the reasonable standards of voice and articulation that he has shown in his prose reading and poetry speaking. He will be relaxed, friendly and courteous, willing to respond to the assessor and to disagree with him (urbanely) if necessary. He will accept an implied invitation to develop a theme, to state a case or rebut an argument. He will speak fluently, logically, coherently and persuasively. On the whole he will avoid the use of slang, although he will not be afraid to use the occasional slang word or phrase where it appears to be the most apt or vital for his purpose.

The teacher-assessor must be on guard against his natural prejudice in favour of the rounded wholeness of the completed sentence.

Quirk has shown that intelligent, well-educated people in good conversation often do not complete a sentence begun.[17] They will often stop and start again with a new grammatical subject, sometimes because they have realized that they have got off on the wrong foot, grammatically speaking, for the best expression of what they have to say. It is clear, says Quirk, that we tend not to talk in 'sentences' at all; the 'sentence' is a term that must be reserved to describe written, not spoken, phenomena. He quotes Fries, 'It is important to recognize that neither the sentence . . . nor the paragraph are units of the living language of speech.'[17] Cherry says the same thing. 'Conversation is rarely "correct" in grammar or syntax; sentences may remain uncompleted, words may be repeated, or phrases uttered several times in different ways.'[6] Furthermore, while economy of speech may be a virtue, the good conversationalist will build-in 'redundancy' (repetitions, stressings, gestures, suggestions of conversational intimacy such as 'you know', 'you see', 'well', 'isn't it?', 'don't you?', etc., and a wealth of other reinforcing 'redundancy') as he judges it to be necessary for the better understanding of his hearer. A good conversation will look very untidy on paper. However, although the speech critic finds many structural defects in good conversation its communicative quality is great indeed.[13]

It is suggested that the following principles should apply to the Conversation item of a test:

(a) The assessor should endeavour to make his share of the conversation as interesting and helpful to the candidate as possible. When the latter is stuck at an awkward pause the assessor should help him along in a friendly way. If it appears that the topic or section of a topic is turning out unsuitably (moving into paths that the assessor is unwilling to pursue, for example) or is patently exhausted the assessor should turn quickly and unobtrusively to another one.

(b) The assessor should ensure that the major share of the talking is done by the candidate.

(c) The conversation should last about five or six minutes.

(d) It should always be the last item in a test.

THE MEASURING SCALE

In the end, effectiveness of any effort to quantify qualitative judgements may depend as much upon the caliber of the judges, and upon their number, as it does upon the specific Rating or Ranking Scale used.[3] Auer, an American speech expert, is here speaking especially of research in speech. The evidence we have from research into the testing of spoken English points clearly to the fact that the source of error is much more likely to be found in the assessor than in any of the other factors in the testing – candidates, material, conditions and the scale of measurement used.

The Americans use various types of measuring scale. Their research has shown that no one technique is much superior to any other (all measuring devices being merely approximations). The two most important, the only ones we need consider, are Ranking and Rating. When ranking is used assessors are asked to place candidates in a rank order, the first rank being assigned to that candidate who appears to the best advantage in the display of the quality or aspect (of speaking, say) to be assessed. In rating assessors are asked to award a mark, which may be literal – A, B, C, D, etc. (A usually being the highest) or numerical (0 and 1 usually being the lowest). With the latter it is, of course, necessary to decide the number of steps, whether 3, 5, 7, 11 or more. If a scale 0–10 is decided on we have an 11-point scale, 10 being the highest mark to be awarded.

Both types of measuring scale have advantages and disadvantages. In ranking the assessor does not need to refer to any general standard he has developed in his assessing outside the particular school in which he finds himself. That is to say, when he is assessing in school 6 he does not have to think – how does this performance compare with what I know of performances in schools, 1, 2, 3, 4, 5? The candidate with Rank 1 will be the best in school 6. On the other hand it does not seem possible for assessors to hold in their minds an order of more than a dozen ranks. If they are asked to rank more than a dozen candidates spurious discriminations may be made – discriminations which are not really felt. Then, if judgements are to be inserted in a record card the rating (numerical or literal) is much more valuable for later reference than the ranking.

There are various objections to rating. In marking a particular group one assessor may rate high (his average mark may be, say, 6), another low (average, say 4); yet their two mark lists might correlate closely. Assessors, or the examining authority, will probably need to add rating marks. But this should be done, in the strict statistical sense, only if the measuring scale is an equal-interval one. No one can possibly say this about any Rating Scale used in a spoken English test. Thurstone points out that in most psychological tests the raw score is merely a numerical index of rank order; there is no defined unit of measurement which can in any fundamental sense be regarded as representing equal increments at the different parts of the scale.[21] In favour of rating it can be said that in practice it is used so widely (especially by teachers in their daily awards of marks in the 'essay-type' of testing) that it ought not to be excluded on theoretical grounds when a choice is to be made between ranking and rating. It can also be said that most American assessors find rating more pleasant than ranking. Ranking and rating are equally reliable. The writer recommends rating.

It is now necessary to decide the number of points on the Rating Scale. Some American speech experts say five only; others use seven, nine or eleven points. The matter really hinges on the ability of assessors to discriminate. How many categories of candidate in a spoken English test can assessors really discriminate? According to recent British research the answer appears to be five. Five should be sufficient for all practical purposes, whether for use on record-cards or on examination certificates. They could denote very good, good, fair, below average, poor; or A, B, C, D, E gradings.

There is, however, a hidden difficulty. It is a quirk of human nature that assessors tend to avoid the extremes of a scale. If assessors of spoken English are asked to use that numerical scale with which every teacher is familiar, the 11-point scale, 0–10, they are unwilling to use the marks 0 and 1 and often 9 and 10; and sometimes even 3 and 8 will not be used. It seems to be thought that 10 represents perfection (of, say, voice) which, of course, no one can attain to, and 0 such an abysmal badness as no candidate could possibly plumb. Even when assessors are encouraged to use the full range – that is to say, to award a 9 or 10 (or a 0 or a 1) where the performance appears to match the descriptions in the Rating Scale – they may use only 6 or 7 points of the scale.

There seem to be two ways of dealing with the problem of 'spread' of marks:

1. If each assessor is to judge a fairly large number of candidates (say, at least a hundred from different schools) then it can be suggested that he follow roughly a given distribution of marks over the entire number. Using an 11-point scale, 0–10 with a mean of 5, a five-point grouping with a normal distribution would be as follows:

	A	B	C	D	E
Marks	0–1	2–3	4–5–6	7–8	9–10
Proportion of candidates	10%	20%	40%	20%	10%

Thus an assessor would aim to get 40 per cent of his candidates in the middle grade and 10 per cent at either end. If all assessors distribute their gradings in this way two desirable results that follow are higher reliability (because the system has forced assessors to use the *entire* five-point scale) and a greater comparability among raters.

We have noted the tendency of assessors to avoid the ends of scales. The tendency to avoid the 'poor' end of the scale (0–1 marks in this case) is greater than the tendency to avoid the 'good' end (9–10), so that there is generally a 'skewing' of the marks towards the 'good' end. Research shows that this happens even when assessors are asked to observe a mathematical distribution about the mean 5. In fact, the actual mean, when the scale 0–10 is operated is nearer to 6 than to 5. The result is that whereas the table shows that a normal distribution would give a total of about 30 per cent of placings in grades D and E the actual percentage one is likely to find is a figure somewhat above or below 20 (with about 15 per cent in Grade D and about 5 per cent in E). If this is how the results turn out it is better to accept them rather than to attempt to reorganize them into a normal distribution. The 'normal distribution' should be a recommendation only.

2. Assessors at the briefing meeting with the chief examiner (discussed later in this chapter) can simply be urged to use the end-marks of the scale 0–10 and to spread their marks as much as possible. It is likely that they will use only 6, 7 or 8 points of the scale. British research suggests that in order to get a true 5-point scale it is necessary to operate an 11-point. With the resulting spread of marks candidates can be grouped into five categories such that the largest (containing the 'average' candidates) is the third, and the fourth and fifth contain about 20 per cent of the total number.

If a school is sharing an examination with a number of other schools in its area it is, of course, possible that its general level of spoken English may be considerably higher than its neighbours'. In this case the assessor will find that he is skewing the whole marking strongly towards the 'good' end. This is inevitable and, indeed, proper. (In any case, the chief examiner will be visiting the school in order to work with the assessor and by a comparison of marks achieve as great a measure of standardization between assessors and schools as possible.) What the writer is here suggesting is that over a number of schools and a large number of candidates the assessor should aim at roughly the sort of distribution suggested. He recommends the use of the 11-point scale, 0–10.

We are now able to proceed with the construction of a Rating Scale. We have decided on an 11-point scale and now need to fit the numerical steps to appropriate descriptions of that aspect or 'detail' we wish to measure. It is recognized practice in America – a practice used in England by P. E. Vernon in the Speech section of his 'General Rating Scale for Qualitative Observations during Testing and Interviewing'[23] – to define only the ends of the continuum of the aspect or quality to be measured. We can for example at the top end of the scale describe 'good' voice and at the other end 'poor' voice fairly fully, leaving the middle ranges undescribed. There is here a continuum of 'pleasantness – unpleasantness' of voice, for there is no distinct division of humanity into those who have, and those

99

who do not have, pleasant voices. A large proportion probably are between the extremes.

We have noted earlier that each observer has in his own perceptual world his own particular version of a speaking performance in the physical world. Assessors are just as individualistic in their interpretations of descriptions and definitions in a Rating Scale. The tighter the definition the less chance there is for individualistic interpretations; the qualities to be rated must be adequately defined. It is not sufficient at one end of the scale to describe, say, the 'power of verbal expression' to which one would allot high marks as 'good' and at the other that to which one would allot low marks as 'poor'. The American Council on Education states that the definition should be as simple as possible, but unambiguous, definite, objective. General terms such as: *very, extremely, average, excellent*, should be avoided. The important point is to establish, as far as possible, an unequivocal meaning.[2] Wilke says the first difficulty which anyone attempting to rate individuals runs up against is the matter of attaching exact and intended meanings to the terms on the Rating Scale.[27] Knower, referring specially to the testing of speech, says that 'terms used in the scale must be precise and meaningful to the observer'.[11] Symonds stresses the importance of definition of qualities to be rated. 'On this hinges much of the success or failure of ratings in general. One of the most potent factors causing unreliability of ratings is ambiguity in meaning of the items on the scale. Every rating is a judgement; judgements depend not only on observation, but also on the interpretation according to certain standards of what is observed. . . . The precision with which the items are described determines the amount of interpretation which the observer needs to make. . . . To reduce the subjectivity of interpretation is the purpose of detailed descriptions of the items to be observed.'[19]

It is a difficult matter to describe qualities or levels in such terms that the assessors who use the scale shall attach meanings sufficiently similar for all practical purposes. The test authority must do all in its power to ensure that its assessors are as nearly of one mind as it is possible for different people to be. This can be done by careful and rigorous briefing, including discussion of questions raised by the assessors. But, first of all, the descriptive terms in the scale must be very carefully chosen.

A Rating Scale that has been rigorously tested in research in schools and colleges will be found in Appendix 2. One section is set out below:

Conversation

Power of Verbal Expression

9 or 10: Lucid, cogent. Well-ordered arrangement of ideas. Spontaneous and fluent command of language. Evidence of capacity to develop a theme. Subject-matter of good quality. Vocabulary suitable and of adequate range. Idiomatic use of language.

7, 8:

4, 5, 6:

2, 3:

0, 1: Finds it difficult to say anything; or is verbose. Ideas are muddled. Meaning unclear. Finds it difficult to develop a theme. Fails to keep to the point. Inadequate vocabulary. Uses slang inappropriately. Poor communication.

This shows the use of a 5-grade scale subdivided to produce 11 steps, with a middle section larger than those on either side. Assessors should be asked to choose, first, one of the grades, and then, second, a point within that grade.

It will be seen that the introduction to the Rating Scale in Appendix 2 contains:

1. A brief statement about the parts of the test and the number of judgements to be made in each.

2. Instructions for operating the Rating Scale.

3. A request that there should be no collaboration between assessors (if there is more than one). It is important that where there is more than one assessor each should make his judgements separately and independently of the others.

4. A warning against Halo (see p. 46).
5. A note on how to deal with the matter of pronunciation.

The lay-out of the assessment sheet is important. An assessor should be able at a glance to make comparisons of the candidates, to see when judging candidate 5 what marks he has awarded to candidates 1, 2, 3, 4. If he uses a separate sheet for each he cannot do this; he must turn back in a flurry of papers. Symonds recommends the use of a 'visible chart', which may be said to keep the advantages of both rating and ranking.[18] The writer suggests a form of visible chart which has been tried in research work and found satisfactory. The following section of this chart makes the lay-out clear:

PROSE READING

	Voice	Articulation	Interpretation
Brown	5	8	4
Jones	7	6	7
Robinson	2	3	6
Smith	9	7	10

It is most important that just before any test in spoken English takes place all assessors should be carefully briefed. This must be done by (a) providing each assessor well in advance of the test with a copy of the Briefing Instructions and a Rating Scale; (b) arranging a meeting with assessors on a day as near as possible to the test in which the chief examiner should take them carefully through the document, discussing definitions and meanings, and answering questions raised by individual assessors. He should describe the scale and instruct the assessors in the marking. They should be asked to attend to 'details' (voice, etc.) separately and deliberately, and to make a separate and deliberate 'General Impression' assessment as the last judgement for each item (Prose Reading, etc.). Assessors should return to the examining authority a set of General Impressions, one for each item in the spoken English test. The chief examiner should caution them against errors such as the 'Halo Effect' and that of 'Central Tendency' (the tendency assessors have to avoid the ends of the scale and bunch their marks in the middle ranges), and advise them on the treatment of pronunciation. He should instruct them in the procedure to be followed and in the method of handling candidates, impressing upon them that procedure and method should be standardized throughout the examination.

This routine should be followed whether the test is an internal school examination, the chief examiner who is to brief the teachers acting as internal assessors being a teacher in the school or a competent assessor perhaps provided by the local education authority, or an examination external to a group of schools for which one or more assessors are to visit each school, the chief examiner being provided by the L.E.A. or some other competent authority.

If possible a few 'guinea-pigs' who have volunteered to undergo a 'dummy test' should be examined, each assessor present taking a turn with a candidate. After all assessors present have recorded their marks and the candidate has left the examination-room the chief examiner should initiate a discussion of the performance and a comparison of the assessment-ratings.

The briefing system just described is a necessary standardizing safeguard. We have seen that assessors tend to disagree somewhat in the marking of any one series of candidates. We should do all we can to minimize this disagreement. We can arrange training sessions for assessors (see Chapter 9); we can devise a Rating Scale expressed in language as clear and unambiguous as possible; we can brief our assessors efficiently, taking them phrase by phrase through the Scale; we can arrange trial 'runs' as part of the briefing system; and we can standardize the system of conducting the actual examination.

There is one further standardizing safeguard we can use. This is to check the marks of each assessor *as they are being awarded* – or rather, some of them. The chief examiner should sit in with each of the other assessors for a part of the latter's working time, making his own assessments of each candidate presented (without revealing them to the assessor concerned). Thus there will be a series of double sets of marks, each set consisting of the chief examiner's assessments and a particular assessor's. The whole series should then be considered. The constant factor is the chief examiner. One assessor's marks may have to be increased in value, another's lowered; a third assessor may prove to be quite out of step – perhaps he may become more reliable with further training, perhaps he must be replaced.

This standardizing safeguard involving the visit of a chief examiner to each of his assessors in turn is suitable for both the 'private' and the 'public' types of oral examination. There is an alternative safeguard which is however suitable only for the 'private' test, and which is considerably more time-consuming. After the marking of all the candidates by its own assessors the school (or other local examining authority – that set up by a group of schools in a particular area, for example) should submit a cross-section (of those with high, moderate and low marks) to a competent external examiner (properly briefed) for reassessment – with subsequent comparison of marks for purposes of moderation.*

SUMMARY

A good test in oral English for schools could comprise some or all of the following items:
1. The reading aloud of a prose passage or passages.
2. The speaking of a poem or short passage of poetry.
3. The giving of a talk.
4. A conversation with the examiner.

Tests now available to schools in England are of two kinds, 'private' (in which nobody is present but candidate and examiner) and 'public' (in which an audience in addition to candidate and examiner is present). The items of examination common to most tests are Prose Reading and Conversation.

* If the number of candidates is so large that a school cannot provide for the testing of everyone it is suggested that after proper briefing interested teachers should be invited to record a speech mark for each of those pupils with whom they have worked for a minimum of, say, six months (a 'pooled' judgement being reached where it is possible to record the judgements of more than one teacher), and thereafter a cross-section only of pupils with recorded high, moderate and low marks submitted to the judgement of a competent external assessor. A comparison of teachers' marks for the cross section with those of the external assessor should provide a good basis for standardization.

Tests should be both valid and reliable. The tests proposed in this book, when conducted by competent assessors under proper conditions, are as valid and reliable as tests of that type of written English most nearly akin, the written essay-type.

It is suggested that the best method of assessment is a combination of the 'general impression' and the 'analytic'. If an overall picture of an item of a speaking performance (say, the giving of a talk) has been gradually built up in the mind of the assessor by the process of judging (and scoring) certain individual 'details' in turn then a final 'general impression' judgement is a stable and reliable one. It is this score which should be returned to an examining authority.

It is suggested that the 'details' for each item of the test should be:

Prose Reading Poetry Speaking	Voice, diction, interpretation, General Impression.
The giving of a Talk	Voice, diction, power of verbal expression, organization and content, General Impression.
Conversation	Voice, diction, power of verbal expression, General Impression.

The source of error in assessment is much more likely to be found in the assessor than in any other of the factors in the testing – candidates, material, and the scale of measurement used.

No one measuring technique is much superior to any other (all measuring devices being merely approximations). The two most important are *Ranking* and *Rating*. Rating is recommended with an 11-point scale, 0–10 (giving a 5-point discrimination).

An assessment sheet in the form of a 'visible chart' is recommended, one in which the assessor can see at a glance all the scores he has so far awarded.

All assessors should be carefully briefed just before a test takes place. If possible they should take part in a 'dummy' test with 'guinea-pig' volunteers.

Assessors should return to the examining authority a set of General Impression marks, one for each item in the oral English test. In addition there could be added for each candidate a brief descriptive statement of his strengths and weaknesses, based on the judging of the individual 'detail' marks.

REFERENCES

1. ALLPORT, G. W. and CANTRIL, H. 'Judging Personality from the Voice.' *J. Soc. Psychol.*, 5, 1934, 37–55.
2. AMERICAN COUNCIL ON EDUCATION. 'The American Council on Education Rating Scale: Its Reliability, Validity and Use.' *Archives of Psychology*, 18, 1930, 18–67.
3. AUER, J. J. *Introduction to Research in Speech*. Harper and Bros., New York, 1959.
4. BECKER, S. L. 'The Rating of Speeches: Scale Independence.' *Speech Monographs*, 29, 1962, 38–44.
5. CAST, B. M. D. 'The Efficiency of Different Methods of Marking English Composition.' *Brit. J. educ. Psychol.*, 9, 1939, 257–69; 10, 1940, 49–60.
6. CHERRY, C. *On Human Communication*. Chapman and Hall, London, 1957.
7. DOUGLAS, J. 'The Measurement of Speech in the Classroom.' *Speech Teacher*, 7, 1958, 309–19.
8. GUILFORD, J. P. *Psychometric Methods*. McGraw-Hill Book Co., New York, 1936.
9. JUDSON, L. S. and WEAVER, A. T. *Voice Science*. Appleton-Century-Crofts, New York, 1942.
10. KNOWER, F. H. 'A Suggestive Study of Public Speaking Rating Scale Values.' *Quarterly J. of Speech*, 15, 1929, 30–41.
11. KNOWER, F. H. 'What is a Speech Test?' *Quarterly J. of Speech*, 30, 485–93, 1944.
12. LANTZ, W. C. 'An Experimental Study of Listeners' Perception of Speech Content as compared with Delivery.' *Abstract in Speech Monographs*, 1956, p. 94.
13. MEERLOO, J. A. M. *Conversation and Communication*. International Universities Press, New York, 1952.

14. MONROE, W. S. *An Introduction to the Theory of Educational Measurement.* Harrap, London, 1922.

15. OLDFIELD, R. C. *The Psychology of the Interview.* Methuen, London, 1951.

16. PERKINS, W. H. 'The Challenge of Functional Disorders of the Voice.' Ch. 26 in *Handbook of Speech Pathology,* ed. Travis, L. E., Peter Owen, London, 1959.

17. QUIRK, R. 'Colloquial English and Communication.' Ch. IX in *Studies in Communication,* ed. Evans, I., Secker and Warburg, London, 1955.

18. SYMONDS, P. M. 'Notes on Rating.' *J. Appl. Psychol.,* 7, 1925, 188–95.

19. SYMONDS, P. M. *Diagnosing Personality and Conduct.* The Century Co., New York and London, 1931.

20. THORNDIKE, R. L. and HAGEN, E. *Measurement and Evaluation in Psychology and Education.* Chapman and Hall, London, 1955.

21. THURSTONE, L. L. *Multiple Factor Analysis.* University of Chicago Press, Chicago, 1947.

22. VALENTINE, C. W. *Psychology and its Bearing on Education.* Methuen, London, 1959.

23. VERNON, P. E. *Personality Tests and Assessments.* Methuen, London, 1953.

24. WATTS, A. F. *Language and Mental Development,* Harrap, 1944.

25. WEAVER, A. T. 'Experimental Studies in Vocal Expression.' *J. Appl. Psychol.,* 8, 1924, 159–86.

26. WEST, R., KENNEDY, L., CARR, A. and BACKUS, O. *The Rehabilitation of Speech.* Harper and Bros., New York and London, 1947.

27. WILKE, W. H. 'Subjective Measurements in Speech: A Note on Method.' *Quarterly J. of Speech,* 21, 1935, 53–9.

28. WISEMAN, S. 'The Marking of English Composition in Grammar School Selection.' *Brit. J. educ. Psychol.,* 19, 1949, 200–9.

29. WOOD, K. S. 'Terminology and Nomenclature'. Ch. 2 in *Handbook of Speech Pathology,* ed. Travis, L. E., Peter Owen, London, 1959.

CHAPTER 7 *Two Types of Test: 'Private' and 'Public'*

We now have a well-designed test in oral English, one that conducted by competent assessors is both valid and reliable. It can be
used as a 'private' or a 'public' test, as a test for internal use only in
the school or as an external test, i.e. as one to be conducted by an
external examining board. It can also be adapted in degree of
difficulty to suit age, intelligence and maturity.

Several ways of using the test are suggested here.

INTERNAL TESTS

(a) A Public type of test for classroom use, i.e. one in which the
candidate has the rest of his class (and perhaps a few interested
teachers) as his audience. This test could be conducted with an
internal examiner, e.g. a specialist teacher of English, or indeed any
member of the school staff with ability and aptitude who has been
properly briefed and given some measure of training by a competent
assessor. The test would comprise *Prose Reading, the giving of a Talk*
and, perhaps, *Poetry Speaking*.

(b) A Private type of test, i.e. a private affair between examiner and
assessor, held in a suitable examination-room in the school. It might
be conducted by an internal assessor or by an external examiner
invited by the school. The test would comprise *Prose Reading,
Conversation* and, perhaps, *Poetry Speaking*.

(c) A test consisting of elements of the Private and Public types, i.e.

the holding of a *Conversation* in private, the giving of a *Talk* to an invited audience, and *Prose Reading* (perhaps with *Poetry Speaking*) either with the *Conversation* in private or with the *Talk* in public.

These three types of test could be very useful for record card purposes.*

EXTERNAL TESTS

(a) A Private or Public type of test conducted in the school by an external examiner appointed by an examining board. (The Associated Board of the Royal Schools of Music and the Guildhall School of Music and Drama would certainly arrange for external examiners to visit schools to conduct 'private' tests, and the English Speaking Board would similarly organize 'public' tests.)

(b) A test, almost certainly of the Private type, conducted by an examining board whose candidates travel to the nearest examination centre.

External tests would of course be conducted in accordance with the examining authorities' regulations and syllabuses.

The really vital differences in the types of test in spoken English lie in the nature of the Private and that of the Public test. These concern both the candidate and the assessor. Many candidates and many assessors are likely to prefer the Private test. Each pair knows that they have complete privacy; this knowledge can bring ease and freedom from tension. Each member of the pair knows that there can be no unfavourable comment from others afterwards, the

---

* It is surely useful for schools to record for each pupil a carefully developed speech mark (with descriptive statement). This has two values: (i) In the form of a brief but clear statement of the strengths and weaknesses of the candidate's oral English it can indicate those aspects of speaking which call for improvement; (ii) Over the years it would be an excellent record of progress and, at the end of school life, a reliable statement of ability in spoken English for use in testimonials, etc. In America it has been shown that the testing procedures the teacher uses certainly help him to arrive at the judgement that is recorded in his mark – an estimate of speech ability. It is probable that in time the assessment of spoken English will in this country become a significant part of the total assessment of pupil or student.

candidate from his friends or teachers, the assessor from other assessors. (It must be borne in mind that the degree of involvement in the test of the assessor who is actually conducting the test is very different from that of an assessor who is a passive observer, and that, because of this vital difference, assessments made by the former may be different from those made by the latter.) In the Public test there may be preoccupation on the part of both candidate and judge with the presence of the audience. Certainly the writer experiences a measure of anxiety due to this preoccupation (perhaps analogous to the anxiety felt by many teachers when one of Her Majesty's Inspectors is present). With experience of testing the anxiety is likely to decrease, but for many assessors it can never be entirely absent. Perhaps it is a function of personality. Extroverts, whether candidates or assessors, are likely to be much happier in the Public test situation than introverts. For the latter the Private test provides the better conditions for the display of those aspects of speaking which are to be tested.

Each form of test has its advantages and disadvantages. Neither is wholly superior to the other. It comes to this – in the school's individual circumstances and for its particular occasions which form, Private or Public, do the authorities prefer? The real value of the proposed test-system lies in its flexibility; it can be adapted to the needs of the school.

CHAPTER 8 *Conducting the Test*

If the test is to be an external one held in the school the examining authority will draw the attention of the school secretary to its regulations and make proposals for test procedure. If the school is holding an internal test, whether Public or Private, it will be necessary to make careful arrangements. This chapter is devoted to suggestions aimed at smoothing and standardizing the procedure. Experience has shown the procedure described here to be efficient and time-saving.

Let us consider first an internal Private test consisting of the two basic items, Prose Reading and Conversation, the minimum time to be allowed for each candidate being ten minutes.

1. Well in advance of the day of the test the topics for conversation should be chosen (either by the assessor or by the candidate – see pp. 93–94) and also the prose passage(s) for reading aloud (chosen by the school testing authority, perhaps a sub-committee with delegated powers). The passage(s) should be typed in pica-type and pasted on a cardboard sheet. A note typed on a small piece of paper should be clipped to the top of the cardboard sheet: 'You have ten minutes in which to look over this reading passage (these reading passages). At the end of that time you will be called into the room where the test is being held and asked to read the passage(s) to the examiner as well as you can.'

2. In good time the assessor (or assessors) should be chosen. It is important that if the assessor is to be a teacher in the school he should not know the candidates too intimately for sober judgement;

he should not take the class or the children very frequently. The elements of novelty and 'occasion' in the testing situation are valuable. The following chapter suggests the personal qualities that go to make a good assessor.

3. Not earlier than the day before the test the assessor (or assessors) should be thoroughly briefed and made familiar with the working of the Rating Scale.

4. Similarly the candidates who are to take the test should be briefed by the member of staff in charge of the test arrangements. It is suggested that this should be done as simply and naturally as possible so that anxiety and 'test-fever' shall be avoided. It is usually only necessary to remind the candidates what the test consists of, to tell them that they will have adequate time to read through their 'unseen' prose and that the conversation with the examiner will be a pleasant experience,* and to inform them of the times at which they must be available. They should be instructed to remind themselves of the timings by looking at the test time-table fixed on the appropriate notice-board.

5. It may not be possible to make any choice of room. If it is possible the following facts should be borne in mind. A good examination-room for our test would be well lit, warm but not too hot, well ventilated, and acoustically not too 'dead' but free from 'boom'. It should be sufficiently large for the candidate and assessor to be separated by about 15 to 18 feet. If there is one available a small room near by should be used as a waiting-room for the next candidate. If not a chair should be placed outside the door of the examination-room.

6. A list of the names of the candidates in examination order should lie on the assessor's desk together with a copy of the Briefing Instructions, some sheets of paper (for note-making), a pencil, rubber, and a duplicated blank mark sheet (see Appendix 2). A clock or watch should be available.

7. It is necessary to prepare a time-table which will show each

* If they have chosen their own subjects of conversation it is as well to remind them of the fact and to suggest that they glance at their notes a little before the test.

candidate the time he is due to appear outside the examination-room to receive his passage(s) of prose for preliminary reading, the time his test is due to start and the time it is due to finish. A section of the time-table for the test might run thus:

CANDIDATE
1.	Jones	Come at 9.30	Start at 9.40	Finish at 9.50 a.m.
2.	Smith	„ „ 9.40	„ „ 9.50	„ „ 10.00 „
3.	Brown	„ „ 9.50	„ „ 10.00	„ „ 10.10 „

This shows that at 9.50 a.m., for example, Candidate No. 1 (Jones) would just have finished his test, Candidate No. 2 (Smith) would be about to start, and No. 3 (Brown) would be ready outside the examination-room door to receive the prose passage(s). No. 2 would be asked to sit on the chair placed next to the point in the examination-room from which he was to read to the examiner, while the latter briefed No. 3 outside the door. This would occupy only a moment. He would hand him a copy of the reading material, ask him whether the instructions attached were quite clear, and tell him that when he had read the passage(s) the assessor would ask him to sit down for a short talk. While No. 2 was being examined No. 3 would be sitting on his chair outside the room (or in a near-by waiting-room) looking over his reading material and considering how best to present it to his audience (the assessor). This procedure, a workable one used many times by the writer, is set down at length because it is important that the flow of candidates should be regular and uninterrupted. It is probably necessary to inform candidates individually of their timings. In any case a copy of the time-table should be displayed on a notice-board the children are in the habit of inspecting.

8. Procedure in the examination-room. (It is important to give the same treatment to each candidate in exactly the same way. The instructions given to the candidate during the course of the test will, of course, be phrased in the assessor's own words. Those used below merely indicate the gist of what should be said. It is, however, important that these instructions should be given to all candidates, and it is a help to standardization if the formula is always used.)

The assessor should now welcome Candidate No. 2. He should ask him to stand at a point (marked on the floor) 18 feet from the centre of the assessor's chair, take his own seat and say to the candidate, 'Please read the first passage *to me* as well as you can.' When he has done this the assessor should say, 'Wait a moment. Start the second passage when you feel you would like to.' (Or, if there is only one passage, 'Please read the passage to me as well as you can.')

At the end of the reading the assessor should say, 'Thank you very much. Now come and sit here.' He should rise and usher the candidate to a second seat placed near the assessor's desk. (This chair should be placed at such a distance and such an angle from the desk as to be near enough for a sense of intimacy in conversation yet far enough away to discourage the candidate from drawing it up to the desk, leaning his elbows on the desk and coming too close to the examiner for the purpose of the test. A convenient arrangement is such that the centre of the candidate's chair is 5 feet away diagonally from the centre of the assessor's chair, with the end of the desk intervening.)

The assessor should end the conversation with Candidate No. 2 just a moment before the expiry of the allotted ten minutes (which in the case of the time-table given as an example above would be 10.0 a.m.), ask him not to discuss the test with other candidates until the end of the examination, thank him for his co-operation and say good-bye. Candidate No. 4 would be waiting to be briefed and Candidate No. 3 to enter the examination-room.

9. The Mark Sheet. A 'visible' mark sheet forms part of Appendix 2. It is suggested that for Prose Reading all 'details' except the General Impression should be marked during the course of the reading aloud, and that the General Impression mark should be awarded immediately the reading is finished. Marks cannot be written down during the course of the Conversation. They should be recorded immediately the conversation is over and before the candidate has left the room, the General Impression mark being awarded last of all. If the school requires it for record card purposes or as a guide to work that should be done with the candidate a brief descriptive statement concerning performance could be jotted down. (This

should cover the strengths and weaknesses of the candidate's oral English.)

10. If the school is conducting its own test (i.e. the test is an internal one) it is suggested that the two General Impression marks should be returned by the assessor to the school authority. These (together with the brief descriptive statement) should also be used for the individual record cards.

If the Private test is to include Poetry Speaking in addition to the two basic items the arrangements outlined above need a simple modification. Fifteen minutes should be ample for the three-item test.

The poetry speaking is to be *prepared*; sufficient time should be allowed for preparation. It is suggested that candidates should have copies of their poems at least a week before the test. As a certain measure of choice of material is to be allowed candidates may well have chosen their poems considerably earlier. At least each should know a week before the test what poem he is to speak. There can be no objection to his getting whatever help is available for preparation.

The time-table will be modified, and the period of waiting will now allow extra time in which the candidate can renew his aesthetic apprehension of his poem.

In the test itself it does not seem to matter whether Prose Reading or Poetry Speaking comes first. It is important that the Conversation should conclude the test. After the first item has been taken the candidate should be invited to sit on the chair placed next to his reading mark, relax for half a minute and study the material of his next piece (Poetry or Prose).

At the end of the test there will of course be three General Impression marks. These can be summed as they are to provide a total mark. If the school test authority feels that a proper balance has not been struck between those parts of the test which provide material for the candidate and that part in which he is to provide his own then the scores for Prose and Poetry can be averaged and the resulting mark added to that for Conversation. It should be pointed out, however, that unseen Prose Reading and prepared Verse Speaking are really very different activities and might well be allowed their full play in a total score.

The internal Public test requires rather different arrangements.

Subjects (or General) topics for the talks or speeches must be chosen well in advance of the day of the test. If the candidates are all members of the same class then the form-room is probably the most convenient examination-room. If they are selected from a number of classes then a room of at least form-room size should be used. It should not be much bigger than this. A very large room such as a school hall can make the test too daunting an affair for many candidates and prevent their achieving their spoken English 'potential'.

The composition of the audience needs to be considered. If the candidates are all members of the same class it is obviously most economical of school-time and causes the least dislocation of the school time-table if each candidate speaks before his or her classmates. We now need a slight adaptation of the time-table procedure as set out on p. 113 for the private test. Let us suppose that we are now dealing with a ten-minute two-item test, consisting of Prose Reading and a Talk. At 9.40 a.m. Candidate No. 1 will be about to begin his test, having spent the previous ten minutes looking at his passage of prose and preparing his talk in an adjoining room or sitting on a chair placed outside the examination room. At this time Candidate No. 2, sitting as a member of the audience, will be asked to accompany the assessor or an administrative assistant out of the room and will be handed the passage(s) of prose to look at and asked to prepare the talk. There will be ten minutes for him to do these things.* At 9.50 a.m. Candidate No. 3 will be ushered out.

* Ten minutes is rather a short space of time in which to read through the prose *and* prepare a talk from material already gathered. It is therefore suggested that the talk in the two-item test be of the easier kind (see p. 89), i.e. the talk on a subject chosen by the candidate and prepared beforehand; in which case the candidate has merely to refresh his memory from his sheet of notes. If the school testing authority wishes to use the type of talk that requires final preparation during the waiting period (i.e. that sort for which the candidate submits a general topic, having prepared background material, the assessor

Whether it be a two- or three-item test there should be a brief interval of relaxation and silence for the candidate between each item and the next. At the end of each item the assessor should invite the candidate to sit on the chair at the latter's table and look over for a minute or so the material for his next item. This brief period of silence allows the candidate to free himself of the influence of the preceding speech activity and to think of the next one (to soak himself in his poem, for example), and the assessor to make his General Impression mark in a moment free from distraction.

---

choosing the actual *subject*) then it is suggested that either of the following courses be adopted: (1) the test be made a three-item examination, in which case fifteen minutes can be allowed for each candidate's examination and consequently fifteen minutes for his waiting period of preparation; (2) *two* ten-minute periods be allowed for preparation. (While this would mean no alteration to the test time-table it would alter each candidate's personal time-table, requiring him to arrive for briefing ten minutes earlier than he would if he were to be allowed only *one* period for preparation.)

CHAPTER 9 *The Examiner*

Good testing depends on the assessor. Research and practical experience both here and in America prove that much more important than the method of judging is the judge himself. Children as candidates in a spoken English test have shown themselves to be fairly stable elements in the testing situation. They tend to give fairly consistent performances; if conditions are good they will produce their best. The real source of 'unreliability' is the assessor. This means that careful thought must be given to the sort of people we need as assessors and the kind of preparation for testing they should undergo.

Knowledge of voice and speech, while a necessary qualification of the assessor, is a subsidiary one. It must take second place to the right sort of personality. Probably the most important personal quality in the examiner – since without it he can never give a candidate the opportunity to realize his full 'potential' – is that described by Oldfield's 'experienced interviewers' who, asked to name 'personal qualities' desirable in the interviewer, variously described a quality recognizable as 'the ability to put people at their ease'.* Among other desirable temperamental qualities (all of which are necessary to the good assessor) they noted 'goodwill', 'an attitude of sympathetic rapport', 'sensitiveness', 'capacity to make other people respond', 'genuine sincerity', 'patience'.[5] Symonds stresses

---

* Knight, writing of intelligence tests, says that 'it is part of the technique of testing to prevent or dissolve emotions and attitudes that spoil a person's performance'.[3]

sincerity and sympathetic understanding, and says that the interviewer must be courteous and deferential, while commanding the respect of his subject without awing him. His position should be one of prestige, but he himself should be friendly and cordial. His personal appearance must be acceptable. He should have a sense of humour.[8] M. D. Vernon notes that 'accurate psycho-physical judgements necessitate the acquired ability on the part of the observer ... to maintain a constant attitude and manner of responding throughout the experimental series'.[9] Knight says that the competent examiner – he is referring to intelligence tests, but what he has to say applies with equal force to tests in spoken English – needs more than the relevant scientific knowledge, he must also possess intelligence, judgement, psychological insight and personal adaptability.[3] He must also be a good listener, in the widest sense of the term. He must attempt an act of communication with his partner in the test. According to Roethlisberger the biggest block to personal communication is man's inability to listen intelligently, understandingly and skilfully to another person.[6]

In order to know a candidate's speech the assessor must, to a certain extent, know the person. At least he knows him better at the end of the test than he did at the beginning. But his knowing him depends on the degree of rapport he has been able to build up during the course of the test. Some assessors, and some people who might be assessors, will be better at 'getting in touch' with candidates than others, and thus in persuading them to give a better speaking performance. Some may find difficulty in getting a conversation going. The Katzes say that in order to get a conversation (with children) started it is necessary to release a certain tension existing between person and person, a tension which can be proved as an actual psychic reality in experience.[2] The tension in the candidate may be the result of excitement, fear or anxiety induced by anticipation of the test, especially perhaps of conversation. It is the business of the assessor to relieve this tension (which may exist not only in the conversation element in the test, but in the prose reading and the other elements – in fact, it may spring into being as the candidate enters the examination-room). If there is obviously a wide disparity in social class between examiner and candidate the child, and perhaps the examiner as well, may feel ill at ease at the beginning of a conversation. The establishment of rapport will consist partly in the examiner's reconciling for the child the two speech patterns brought to the conversation. (With many persons a conversation in an unfamiliar speech pattern is experienced as a conflict.)[4] If the examiner is unskilful the two parties to the conversation may not be able to establish real contact. If hostility develops the test is bound to be a failure. But once the conversation is felt to be a pleasant experience reserve and suspicion are dissipated; both parties lose their rigidity and the optimum conditions are established for the candidate to achieve his 'potential'.

Honesty is an important quality of character in the assessor who is judging spoken English tests. The assessor will be inspired by ideals of duty; but his judgement is not likely to be questioned officially and he can be as careful or as careless as he likes. Wolters says that in the end accurate observation is largely the result of moral qualities. It depends upon *honest* effort. The moral factors, of course, require the backing of systematic knowledge.[10]

To sum up the personal qualities and abilities of a good assessor we can say that, in addition to sound technical knowledge, he should have a warm and friendly personality, that he should be sincerely interested in people as well as in speech, that he should have no difficulty in establishing good relations with the candidate, that he should have the self-knowledge to enable him to know what effect he is having on the candidate, that he should have the ability to adjust his examination technique to the pace and the intelligence of the candidate and to maintain a constant attitude and manner of responding throughout the examination series, and that he should be a good listener. His personal integrity should be beyond question.

The personal qualities enumerated are just those qualities with which good teachers are endowed. It is clear that in many schools teachers must be asked to conduct the tests in spoken English; it is probable that many teachers will want to do so. If their judgements are to be reliable they must be prepared for the task. The writer suggests that the minimum preparation should consist of two or three briefing sessions, part of the last of which should be devoted to a 'live' practice run with volunteer guinea-pig candidates. Further useful work could be done in a session with 'taped' performances in which the potential assessors could be asked to make judgements using the Rating Scale, after which a discussion of the results would be led by a trained assessor. Teachers of Speech and Drama are increasingly to be found on the staffs of the larger secondary schools, especially of comprehensive schools. These should make admirable chief examiners who could take charge of the briefing sessions, including the 'live' and 'taped' practice runs. For other schools a visiting specialist might be made available by the local education authority.

It is suggested that the first session (or two sessions if two should be necessary) should be devoted to a talk or lecture-discussion dealing with the background to testing – the nature of measurement, the making of judgements, etc. – the last to briefing for the testing, i.e. instruction on the scoring and the conduct of the test.

Let us consider the work to be done in the earlier sessions. Potential assessors must become aware of the factors involved in the making of judgements about speech performances. It is suggested that the material of Chapter 5 would form a good basis for a discussion led by the chief examiner or the visiting specialist. Bound up in a consideration of the nature of judgement-making will be the nature of subjective measurement. The scores arrived at will be the result of careful observation; but, as we have seen in Chapter 5, observation is a highly personal matter, and each individual observes in his own individual way. Each performance to be measured must be a performance-as-observed, and any one assessor's performance-as-observed will to a greater or lesser degree be different from any other assessor's. Douglas puts it thus: 'All scores, observations, judgements, grades are approximations – part of the score is due to the thing we are trying to measure and part of it is due to the observation or testing process itself.'[1]

The chief examiner will try in these sessions to give the trainee-assessors some understanding of the determinants of perception and of the explosive nature of the relationship between the examiner and the candidate. He will deal also with the complexity and the unitary nature of the speech act and the difficulties involved in making judgements on a basis of fragmentation (pointing to a satisfactory solution in the built-up 'General Impression' judgement, a Gestalt which is much more than the sum of its parts). And he will raise the problem of *standards* for discussion.

It is unlikely that many assessors have a background knowledge of the concepts of statistics basic to their testing. It would be useful to potential assessors if in the preliminary sessions the discussion-leader were to examine with them the concepts of validity and reliability. (A useful beginning could be made with a discussion of the matter of Chapter 6, pp. 62–65.) It could be suggested that potential assessors should become familiar with the basic concepts of dispersion, distribution, standard deviation, normal curve, sampling. (These can be studied in any good book dealing with statistics for schools, e.g. Sumner, *Statistics In School*.)[7]

The second part of the final session should be devoted to a practice test with volunteer candidates. During each candidate's performance assessors should record their marks privately; after the performance there should be a comparison and discussion of assessments. This will mean a delay of several minutes between candidates. In the first part of this final session the chief examiner should brief the potential assessors as though they were about to conduct a real examination. A suggested plan for this briefing has been set out on pp. 102–103.

If there is time further work could be done with 'taped' recordings. After each candidate's performance there should be a comparison and discussion of assessments.

The work-sessions just described seem to the writer to be the minimum training-briefing that a teacher interested in the testing of spoken English should undergo. They will at least make him aware of the grounds upon which his decisions rest and of the sources of error in his judgements, show him how to conduct a test and give him some supervised practice in testing.

REFERENCES

1. DOUGLAS, J. 'The Measurement of Speech in the Classroom.' *Speech Teacher*, 7, 1958, 309–19.
2. KATZ, D. and KATZ, R. *Conversations with Children*. Kegan Paul, London, 1936.
3. KNIGHT, R. *Intelligence and Intelligence Tests*. Methuen, London, 1953.
4. MEERLOO, J. A. M. *Conversation and Communication*. International Universities Press, New York, 1952.
5. OLDFIELD, R. C. *The Psychology of the Interview*. Methuen, London, 1951.
6. ROETHLISBERGER, F. J. 'Barriers to Communication between Men.' *Review of General Semantics*, 9, 1952, 89–93.
7. SUMNER, W. L. *Statistics in School*. Blackwell, Oxford, 1958.
8. SYMONDS, P. M. *Diagnosing Personality and Conduct*. The Century Company, New York and London, 1931.
9. VERNON, M. D. *A Further Study of Visual Perception*. The University Press, Cambridge, 1952.
10. WOLTERS, A. W. P. *The Evidence of Our Senses*. Methuen, London, 1933.

Appendices

Appendices

Sample Passages of Prose and Poetry for Oral Interpretation

(a) *Linked passages (with suggested questions to follow the reading as a lead-in to Conversation)*

1. *An English Conductor*

An English conductor, who was touring with a famous British orchestra in Hungary, made a habit of announcing the titles of the various items in English. Not 2 per cent of his listeners understood him, but he felt that his occasional speaking established an atmosphere of friendliness which would have been lost had he merely stood with his back to them and conducted.

On one occasion he announced, 'We are now going to play an overture by a contemporary British composer, Dr. Vaughan Williams.' The audience listened in polite and friendly seriousness. Then he added, 'It is called – "The Wasps".'

At once the seriousness vanished. Titters came from all parts of the hall. 'Sps!' said someone. 'Sps!' And immediately all and sundry began delightedly practising the strange combination: Sps! Sps! Sps! 'Strange sound!' they were plainly saying. 'What a language!' 'Did you ever hear anything quite like that? Sps!'

It was five minutes before the performance could begin, but it need hardly be said that, when it did, it was a success from first note to last.

1. *The Octopus*

Then the creeping murderer, the octopus, steals out, slowly, softly, moving like a grey mist, pretending now to be a bit of weed, now a rock, now a lump of decaying meat, while its evil goat eyes watch coldly. It oozes and flows towards a feeding crab, and as it comes close, its yellow eyes burn and its body turns rosy with the pulsing colour of anticipation and rage. Then suddenly it runs lightly on the tips of its arms as ferociously as a charging cat. It leaps savagely on the crab, there is a puff of black fluid, and the struggling mass is obscured in the sepia cloud. On the exposed rocks out of the water the barnacles bubble behind their closed doors and the limpets dry out. And down to the rocks come the black flies to eat anything they can find.

(i) Which passage do you prefer? (Why?)

OR

(ii) Can you mention one big difference between the two passages?
(iii) Is there, do you think, any difference between listening to an orchestra on the wireless and listening to it in the concert hall? (What differences?)
(iv) Is the second passage a scientific description of an octopus? (If not, why not?)

OR

(v) What does the writer feel about the octopus?
(vi) Are variations of pace in reading aloud desirable in 'The Octopus'? (Where, why?)

2. *The Nature of Scientific Prose*

Many men and women, since the waters of the deluge disappeared from the face of the earth, have looked at rainbows and have described them in many phrases, evoked by a sense of beauty and wonderment. These sensations are not noticeable when the physicist says '. . . the observer stands with his back to the sun, and all raindrops at about 42 degrees to the line joining the sun to his head appear red and those at about 40 degrees appear violet. These form the primary bow. For the secondary bow the angular radius of the red is about 51 degrees and of the blue 54·5 degrees.' No doubt this is an accurate statement of the principles underlying the formation of the rainbow, but it is hard to avoid the impression that something, some thing that appealed to Noah, is missing.

2. An Incident of the Great Frost: the King's Carnival

Near London Bridge, where the river had frozen to a depth of some twenty fathoms, a wrecked wherry boat was plainly visible, lying on the bed of the river where it had sunk last autumn, overladen with apples. The old bumboat woman, who was carrying her fruit to market on the Surrey side, sat there in her plaids and farthingales with her lap full of apples for all the world as if she were about to serve a customer, though a certain blueness about the lips hinted the truth. 'Twas a sight King James specially liked to look upon, and he would bring a troupe of courtiers to gaze with him. In short, nothing could exceed the brilliancy and gaiety of the scene by day. But it was at night that the carnival was at its merriest. For the frost continued unbroken; the nights were of perfect stillness; the moon and stars blazed with the hard fixity of diamonds, and to the fine music of flutes and trumpets the courtiers danced.

(The Nature of Scientific Prose)

(i) What is the something that appealed to Noah that is missing from the 'accurate statement of the principles underlying the formation of the rainbow'? Is it possible to make such a statement which will include the 'something'?

(ii) Is the prose used in scientific writing different from the prose used in other sorts of writing? If so, in what way is it different? Should it be different?

OR

Is there such a form of writing as scientific prose? (If so, what are its characteristics? And what other sorts of prose-writing are there?)

(iii) What does the word 'prose' mean to you?

(An Incident of the Great Frost: the King's Carnival)

(i) Are there any indications that this is a piece of fiction-writing? (If so, what are they?)

(ii) Is there any suggestion of poetry in this piece of prose? (If so, what?)

3. *The Spirit of Science*

You know how fond the scientist is of drawing graphs – well, imagine our drawing some graphs of the very best man could accomplish along various lines at different times in history. Take travel, for instance. For tens of thousands of years, until almost within living memory, the fastest he could travel was limited by the speed of a horse on land, a sailing ship on the sea. Now, an aeroplane crosses land and sea fifty times as fast. Take the rate at which news could travel. The news of Nelson's victory at Aboukir, a very important historical event, took two months to reach England from Egypt, and the news of Trafalgar took a fortnight. Now, telegraph, telephone, and radio are almost instantaneous, so that we can read in the evening paper of a battle which took place in the Pacific the same morning. For power, man used to depend on his own muscles or those of animals: think of all the power we now have at our disposal. It would require two million horses, for instance, to provide a steady output of energy equal to that of the completed Battersea Power Station alone. Or craftsmanship: compare the rate at which things can now be made as compared with a hundred years ago. All our graphs, after running almost flat for ten thousand years, have suddenly in the last century taken a tremendous upward turn and are still going up steeply.

From a broadcast on 'The Spirit of Science' by
Sir Lawrence Bragg

3. *Memories of Christmas*

In goes my hand into that wool-white bell-tongued ball of holidays resting at the margin of the carol-singing sea, and out comes Mrs Prothero and the firemen.

It was on the afternoon of the day of Christmas Eve, and I was in Mrs Prothero's garden, waiting for cats, with her son Jim. It was snowing. It was always snowing at Christmas; December, in my memory, is white as Lapland, though there were no reindeers. But there were cats. Patient, cold, and callous, our hands wrapped in socks, we waited to snowball the cats. Sleek and long as jaguars and terrible-whiskered, spitting and snarling they would slink and sidle over the white back-garden walls, and the lynx-eyed hunters, Jim and I, fur-capped and moccasined trappers from Hudson's Bay off Eversley Road, would hurl our deadly snowballs at the green of their eyes. The wise cats never appeared. We were so still, Eskimo-footed arctic marksmen in the muffling silence of the eternal snows – eternal, ever since Wednesday – that we never heard Mrs Prothero's first cry from her igloo at the bottom of the garden. Or, if we heard it at all, it was, to us, like the far-off challenge of our enemy and prey, the neighbour's Polar Cat. But soon the voice grew louder. 'Fire!' cried Mrs Prothero, and she beat the dinner-gong. And we ran down the garden, with snowballs in our arms, towards the house, and smoke indeed was pouring out of the dining-room, and the gong was bombilating, and Mrs Prothero was announcing ruin like a town-crier in Pompeii. This was better than all the cats in Wales standing on the wall in a row. We bounded into the house, laden with snowballs, and stopped at the open door of the smoke-filled room.

Dylan Thomas, *Quite Early One Morning*

(i) Which passage do you prefer? Why?

(ii) The two pieces move at very different speeds. Which is steadier? Which accelerates and where?

(iii) Are there any disadvantages in the picture of speed and mass production drawn by Bragg?

(iv) What do you think of the first sentence in the extract by Dylan Thomas?

(v) What do you think should be the main characteristic of scientific prose?

(b) *Fairly Easy Passages*

4. *Leisure*

Too often today we hear people complain of being bored. With the changes in the nature of work and leisure that greater technical skill and knowledge have brought has come frustration. We know that Man needs to create if he is to be contented, but it is only the machine that creates today – man is a machine-minder. Even in the kitchen, gadgets do most of the work. People therefore are often deprived of the pleasure of doing something for themselves.

Even our hobbies have been attacked by the machine age. Instead of making models we fix together prefabricated kits; instead of playing a musical instrument we play records. We take our pleasures passively and are rapidly becoming a nation of watchers and listeners.

Television is the villain of the piece. In front of it we sit for hours, gazing glassily at the flickering screen, watching almost anything that is broadcast. We stop thinking, stop talking, stop everything to watch the monster. Very quickly we lose the will to create, for watching is so easy. With television we pass time, we do not use it.

Today more and more leisure is becoming available to us as automation develops – but fewer and fewer of us know how to use our extra time profitably. We need more training for leisure in schools, more centres for social activities, and a drastic revision of television programmes so that they are more stimulating and per-suade us to go off and do something for ourselves.

5. Fashion

We are too concerned with fashion. At least, the ladies are. Is it really a good thing to be 'different' – if you are merely following the lead of a film star or taking a hint from the beauty pages of a maga-zine? Think of the money and time it takes to be 'up to date'. Clothes are discarded before they show a sign of wear; hair-styles and colours seem to change from day to day. We are no sooner used to mauve-tinted hair heaped high on the head than we find that fashion says hair should be worn straight and rough as though it has not been combed. Whatever the style you may be sure it will take ages to arrange it.

So far this century most men have not been affected so greatly by fashion – except when they have to pay for women's clothes. Now it seems that men's clothes must keep up to date too. The sober-coloured, sensible suit that has been man's 'uniform' so long is giving way to new colours, new materials and new styles. We already hear of 'male models'. How long will it be before men, too, must study magazines and worry about being seen wearing last year's casual jacket? For one thing, at least, we can be thankful – not many men over the age of fifty will be worried about changing hair-styles.

6. *Mij, the Otter*

There was only one incident that evening; an incident, however, that for a moment looked like bringing the whole train to a stop. It had not occurred to me that Mij could, in that very small space, get into any serious mischief; it had not crossed my mind, for example, that by standing on the piled luggage he could reach the communication cord. This, however, was precisely what he had done, and when my eye lit on him he already had it firmly between his teeth while exploring with his paws the tunnel into which its ends disappeared. It was probably nothing but this curiosity as to detail that had so far saved the situation; now as I started towards him he removed his fingers from the hole and braced them against the wall for the tug. It takes a surprisingly strong pull to ring the communication bell, but Mij had the strength, and, it seemed, the will. I caught him round the shoulders, but he kept his grip, and as I pulled him I saw the chain bulge outward; I changed my tactics and pushed him towards it, but he merely braced his arms afresh. Suddenly I knew what to do. Mij was extremely ticklish, particularly over the ribs; I began to tickle him, and at once his jaws relaxed into the foolish grin that he kept for such occasions and he began to squirm. Later that evening he tried several times to reach the cord again, but by then I had rearranged the suitcases, and it was beyond the furtherest stretch of his elastic body.

Gavin Maxwell, *Ring of Bright Water*

7. *Mr Pickwick on the Ice*

The sport was at its height, the sliding was at the quickest, the laughter was at the loudest, when a sharp, smart crack was heard. There was a quick rush towards the bank, a wild scream from the ladies, and a shout from Mr Tupman. A large mass of ice disappeared, the water bubbled up over it, and Mr Pickwick's hat, gloves and handkerchief were floating on the surface; and this was all of Mr Pickwick that anybody could see.

Dismay and anguish were depicted on every countenance; the males turned pale, and the females fainted; Mr Snodgrass and Mr Winkle grasped each other by the hand, and gazed at the spot where their leader had gone down, with frenzied eagerness; while Mr Tupman, by way of rendering the promptest assistance, and at the same time conveying to any persons who might be within hearing, the clearest possible notion of the catastrophe, ran off across the country at his utmost speed, screaming 'Fire!' with all his might and main.

At this very moment a face, head, and shoulders emerged from beneath the water, and disclosed the features and spectacles of Mr Pickwick.

After a vast quantity of splashing, and cracking, and struggling, Mr Pickwick was at length fairly extricated from his unpleasant position, and once more stood on dry land.

Charles Dickens, *Pickwick Papers*

8. *The Ascent of Everest*

The ridge continued as before. Giant cornices on the right, steep rock slopes on the left. I went on cutting steps on the narrow strip of snow. The ridge curved away to the right and we had no idea where the top was. As I cut around the back of one hump, another higher one would swing into view. Time was passing and the ridge seemed never-ending. In one place, where the angle of the ridge had eased off, I tried cramponing without cutting steps, hoping this would save time, but I quickly realized that our margin of safety on these steep slopes at this altitude was too small, so I went on step-cutting. I was beginning to tire a little now. I had been cutting steps continuously for two hours, and Tenzing, too, was moving very slowly. As I chipped steps around still another corner, I wondered rather dully just how long we could keep it up. Our original zest had now quite gone and it was turning more into a grim struggle. I then realized that the ridge ahead, instead of still monotonously rising, now dropped sharply away, and far below I could see the North Col and the Rongbuk Glacier. I looked upwards to see a narrow snow ridge running up a snowy summit. A few more whacks of the ice-axe in the firm snow and we stood on top.

Sir John Hunt, *The Ascent of Everest*

9. *Pinocchio*

At first Pinocchio tried to pluck up heart a little, but when it really came home to him that he was imprisoned in the body of a seamonster he began weeping and shrieking, and as he wept he yelled, 'Help! help! Oh poor me! Will no one come to my rescue?'

'Whoever would want to rescue you, you wretch?' came a voice from the darkness. It sounded like a guitar out of tune.

'Who can it be, speaking like that?' cried Pinocchio, feeling himself freeze with terror.

'Me! I'm a poor Tunny, swallowed by the Dogfish at the same time as you. What sort of a fish are you?'

'I'm nothing to do with fish: I'm a marionette.'

'Well, if you're not a fish, how did you get yourself swallowed by a sea-monster?'

'I didn't get myself swallowed. He just swallowed me! But what shall we do now in all this darkness?'

'Make up our minds to wait till the Dogfish has digested both of us!'

'But I don't want to be digested,' howled Pinocchio.

'No more do I want to be digested,' went on the Tunny, 'but I am something of a philosopher, enough to console myself by thinking that when one is born a Tunny it's more becoming to die in water than in oil!'

'Beastly nonsense!' screamed Pinocchio.

'That, however, is my opinion,' replied the Tunny; 'and opinions, as our politician Tunnies say, always deserve respect.'

'Anyhow, I want to get out of this. I want to escape.'

'Escape then, if you *can* get out.'

'Is this Dogfish which has swallowed us very big?' asked th
puppet.

'You can reckon that the body is somewhere about a mile long
not counting the tail.'

Charles Collodi, *Pinocchi*

10. The Flying Fool

I shake myself violently, ashamed of my weakness, alarmed at my
inability to overcome it. I never before understood the meaning o
temptation, or how powerful one's desires can become. I've got to
alert my mind, wake my body. I can't let anything as trifling a
sleep ruin the flight I spent so many months in planning. How could
I ever face my partners and say that I failed to reach Paris because
I was sleepy? No matter how inaccurate my navigation, it must be
the best I can carry on. Honour alone demands that. The more my
compasses swing, the more alert I must stay to compensate for their
errors. If my plane can stay aloft, if my engine can keep on running
then so can I.

I cup my hand into the slipstream, diverting a strong current o
air against my face, breathing deeply of its gusty freshness. I let my
eyelids fall shut for many seconds; then raise them against tons o
weight. Protesting, they won't open wide until I force them with
my thumb, and lift the muscles of my forehead to help keep them in
place. Sleep overcomes my resistance like a drug.

My fingers are cold from the slipstream. I draw my mitten
on again. Shall I put on flying boots? But I'd have to unbuckle
the safety-belt and take my feet off the rudder pedals, and do
most of the work with one hand. The *Spirit of St. Louis* would
veer off course and I'd have to straighten it out a dozen times
before I got the boots on. It's too much effort. I'd rather be a little
cold.

Colonel Charles Lindberg, *The Spirit of St. Louis*

11. The Net

'Something checked us. Not with a jolt, but with a gentle yielding,
and a slight rubbing sound. From where I sat in the stern of the

136

dinghy, keeping a little way on, and steering with a muffled oar, I could see practically nothing in the darkness, but it did not feel as if we had hit the bank.

'What is it?' I whispered.

The little boat rocked as Phyllis clambered forward. There was a faint thud from some part of our gear dislodged. Presently her whisper came back.

'It's a net. A big one.'

'Can you lift it?'

She shifted. The dinghy rocked again, and then remained tilted for a moment. It relaxed back to an even keel.

'No. Too heavy,' she said.

I hadn't expected that kind of hold-up. A few hours before in daylight I had prospected the route with binoculars, from a church tower. I had observed that to the north-west there was a narrow gap between two hills, and that beyond it the water widened out into a lake stretching farther than I could see. It looked as if, once past that neck, one ought to be able to travel a considerable distance without coming too close to the shore. I traced the way to the gap and memorized it with care before I came down. The tide turned and began to rise before it was quite dark. We waited another half-hour, and then set off, rowing up on the flood. It had not been too difficult to find the gap, for the silhouette of the two hills showed faintly against the sky. I had moved to the stern to steer and let the tide carry us silently through. And now there was the net. . . .

I turned the craft so that the flow held us broadside against the barrier. I shipped the oar cautiously, felt for the net, and found it. It was made of half-inch rope with about a six-inch mesh, I judged. I felt for my knife.

"Hold on," I whispered. "I'll cut a hole.'"

John Wyndham, *The Kraken Wakes*

12. *Memoirs of a Sword Swallower*

I knew if I was going to swallow them I'd have to do it at once before they got too warm. If you swallow a hot tube, it will stick to your insides and you can't withdraw it. So I picked up the red tube and while the Impossible watched me with deep interest, I wiped it with a cloth as I would a sword I was about to swallow. This had become an instinctive reaction. I still had an instant's nervousness before swallowing a sword, and wiping it gave me a couple of seconds to get up my confidence.

I stood with my head thrown back and the tube held straight up from my lips. I held it by the electrical connections with my right hand and with my cupped left I guided it down my throat. The basic principle of sword-swallowing is to establish a straight line from the throat to the stomach and with the delicate glass tube I made a special effort to hold myself as straight as possible. As the tube slid down, it was pleasantly warm, unlike the chill of steel, but terribly wide. I had to force it a little as it began its descent.

I felt the tube hit my breast-bone. I'd had this happen with swords. It's always a creepy feeling, for it sends a shudder all through you. Very often even a slight blow will bruise the bone so it aches afterwards. I can only describe the feeling as similar to a sharp blow on the solar plexus in boxing, but you'd have to experience the sensation yourself to understand it. The tip of the tube slid off the bone and glided down smoothly until my right hand, holding the electrical connections of the tube, touched my lips.

I withdrew the tube and turned round to the Impossible. 'Did it shine through my chest?' I asked anxiously.

'M'boy, you shone up like a jack-o'-lantern,' he assured me respectfully. 'It's a lovely act. I was very nearly taken sick myself!'

Dan Mannix, Memoirs of a Sword-Swallower

13. *Syler's Green: A Return Journey*

When I was promoted to the Transition Class, life seemed even more wonderful. We were told the story of Beowulf and how he tore off Grendel's arm in the depths of the lake (and this tale we used of course to play later in the woods and by the great lake in Scapelands Park); and above all we were learning in our geography lessons about the tropics. Oh those tropics, how much I loved them (although I had and still have a horror of snakes). But our form-mistress who combined geography with painting – and subsequently left us for ever to study Egyptology under Flinders Petrie and go out digging with him to Egypt – had a real gift for bringing the jungle home to a young child of tender years.

'Now, children,' she would say, 'have you got any large hat-boxes or dress-boxes at home?'

Yes, yes, our mamas had plenty of such boxes.

'Then bring them along with you tomorrow, and bring some moss to lay flat in the bottom of the box and then we can begin with our jungle scene.'

The next day we would set to work in earnest. With rich indigoes and blues and ochres and greens we would slosh the inside of the box until it looked, to our inspired imagination (inspired by our mistress's description), exactly like the jungle and the tropical forest scene. And in this jungle would crawl and fly and climb and jabber and whine and shriek all the animals, birds, and reptiles we had heard about, and seen in visits to the zoo, and seen in the bright pictures our mistress used to hand round.

This school was extremely strong in history, literature, and geography but I fear it was an unorthodox education and today would be frowned upon.

From a broadcast by Stevie Smith

14. *A Wedding Present*

One Saturday previously I had taken several of the children into Caxley to buy Miss Gray's wedding present for which the whole school had been collecting for weeks. I had managed to assemble all the children together, sending Miss Gray to the post office for more saving stamps. This manœuvre was considered highly daring and the children were in a conspiratorial mood during her short absence, Eric going so far as to keep watch at the lobby door while we made our plans.

It was decided, in hushed whispers, that a piece of china would be appreciated, and the deputation, under my guidance, were given powers to make the final choice, not however without plenty of advice.

'Something real good! Like you'd want for always!'

'And pretty too. Not some ol' pudden basin, say. A jam dish, more like!'

'Flowers, and that, on it . . . see?'

We promised to do what we could just as Eric thrust an agitated countenance round the door, saying:

'She's coming!'

With many secret giggles and winks they dispersed to their desks and all was unnaturally quiet when Miss Gray entered and handed over the saving stamps.

'What very good children,' she remarked; and then looked amazed at the gale of laughter that this innocent remark had released.

In Johnson's shop at Caxley, the business of choosing the present was undertaken seriously. We surveyed jam dishes, desssert services, and fruit bowls, and I had great difficulty in steering them away from several distressing objects highly reminiscent of Mrs Pratt's collection. One particularly loathsome teapot fashioned like a wizened pumpkin exerted such a fascination over the whole party that I feared Miss Gray might have to cherish it under Mr Annett's roof, but luckily, the man who was attending to us, with most commendable patience, brought out a china biscuit barrel, sprigged with wild flowers. It was useful, it was very pretty, and it was exactly the right price. We had returned to Fairacre, after ices all round in a teashop, very well content with our purchase.

'Miss Read', *Village School*

(c) *More Difficult Passages*

15. *Indian Summer of a Forsyte*

It was quite shady under the tree; the sun could not get at him, only make the rest of the world bright so that he could see the Grand Stand at Epsom away out there, very far, and the cows cropping the clover in the field and swishing at the flies with their tails. He smelled the scent of limes, and lavender. Ah! that was why there was such a racket of bees. They were excited – busy, as his heart was busy and excited. Drowsy, too, drowsy and drugged on honey and happiness; as his heart was drugged and drowsy. Summer – summer – they seemed saying; great bees and little bees, and the flies, too.

The stable clock struck four; in half an hour she would be here. He would have just one tiny nap, because he had had so little sleep of late; and then he would be fresh for her, fresh for youth and beauty, coming towards him across the sunlit lawn – lady in grey! And settling back in his chair he closed his eyes. Some thistledown came on what little air there was, and pitched on his moustache, more white than itself. He did not know; but his breathing stirred it, caught there. A ray of sunlight struck through and lodged on his boot. A bumble-bee alighted and strolled on the crown of his Panama hat. And the delicious surge of slumber reached the brain beneath that hat, and the head swayed forward and rested on his breast. Summer – summer! So went the hum.

The stable clock struck the quarter past. The dog Balthasar stretched and looked up at his master. The thistledown no longer moved. The dog placed his chin over the sunlit foot. It did not stir. The dog withdrew his chin quickly, rose, and leaped on old Jolyon's lap, looked in his face, whined; then, leaping down, sat on his haunches, gazing up. And suddenly he uttered a long, long howl.

But the thistledown was still as death, and the face of his old master.

Summer – summer – summer! The soundless footsteps on the grass!

John Galsworthy, The Forsyte Saga

16. *The Pleasure of Painting*

Some experiments one Sunday in the country with the children's paint-box led me to procure the next morning a complete outfit for painting in oils.

Having bought the colours, an easel, and a canvas, the next step was to begin. But what a step to take! The palette gleamed with beads of colour; fair and white rose the canvas; the empty brush hung poised, heavy with destiny, irresolute in the air. My hand seemed arrested by a silent veto. But after all the sky on this occasion was unquestionably blue, and a pale blue at that. There could be no doubt that blue paint mixed with white should be put on the top part of the canvas. One really does not need to have had an artist's training to see that. It is a starting-point open to all. So very gingerly I mixed a little blue paint on the palette with a very small brush, and then with infinite precaution made a mark about as big as a bean upon the affronted snow-white shield. It was a challenge, a deliberate challenge; but so subdued, so halting, indeed so cataleptic, that it deserved no response. At that moment the loud approaching sound of a motor-car was heard in the drive. From this chariot there stepped swiftly and lightly none other than the gifted wife of Sir John Lavery. 'Painting! But what are you hesitating about? Let me have a brush – the big one.' Splash the turpentine, wallop into the blue and the white, frantic flourish on the palette – clean no longer – and then several large, fierce strokes and slashes of blue on the absolutely cowering canvas. Anyone could see that it could not hit back. No evil fate avenged the jaunty violence. The canvas grinned in helplessness before me. The spell was broken. The sickly inhibitions rolled away. I seized the largest brush and fell upon my victim with berserk fury. I have never felt any awe of a canvas since.

Winston Churchill

17. *Anatomy of a Crime*

'The deed was executed with a degree of steadiness and self-possession equal to the wickedness with which it was planned. The circumstances now clearly in evidence spread out the scene before us. Deep sleep had fallen upon the intended victim and all beneath his roof. A healthful old man to whom sleep was sweet, the first sound slumbers of the night held him in their soft but strong embrace. The assassin enters, through a window already prepared, into an unoccupied apartment. With noiseless foot he paces the lonely hall, half-lighted by the moon; he winds up the ascent of the stairs, and reaches the door of the chamber. Of this, he moves the lock by soft and continued pressure, till it turns on its hinges without noise; and he enters, and beholds the victim before him. The room is uncommonly open to the admission of light. The face of the innocent sleeper is turned from the murderer, and the beams of the moon, resting on the gray locks of the aged temple, show him where to strike. The fatal blow is given! and the victim passes, without a struggle or a motion, from the repose of sleep to the repose of death! It is the assassin's purpose to make sure work; and he plies the dagger, though it is obvious that life has been destroyed by the blow of the bludgeon. He even raises the aged arm, that he may not fail in his aim at the heart, and replaces it again over the wounds of the poniard! To finish the picture, he explores the wrist for the pulse! He feels for it, and ascertains that it beats no longer! It is accomplished. The deed is done. He retreats, retraces his steps to the window, passes out through it as he came in, and escapes. He has done the murder. No eye has seen him, no ear has heard him. The secret is his own, and it is safe!'

Daniel Webster

18. *Silas and Eppie*

It was not until Silas had carried her home, and begun to think of the necessary washing, that he recollected the need that he should punish Eppie, and 'make her remember'. The idea that she might run away again and come to harm gave him unusual resolution, and for the first time he determined to try the coal-hole – a small closet near the hearth.

'Naughty, naughty Eppie,' he suddenly began, holding her on his knee, and pointing to her muddy feet and clothes – 'naughty to cut with the scissors and run away. Eppie must go into the coal-hole for being naughty. Daddy must put her in the coal-hole.'

He half-expected that this would be shock enough, and that Eppie would begin to cry. But instead of that, she began to shake herself on his knee, as if the proposition opened a pleasing novelty. Seeing that he must proceed to extremities, he put her into the coal-hole, and held the door closed, with a trembling sense that he was using a strong measure. For a moment there was silence, but then came a little cry, 'Opy, opy!' and Silas let her out again, saying, 'Now, Eppie 'ull never be naughty again, else she must go in the coal-hole – a black, naughty place.'

The weaving must stand still a long while this morning, for now Eppie must be washed, and have clean clothes on; but it was to be hoped that this punishment would have a lasting effect, and save time in future – though, perhaps, it would have been better if Eppie had cried more.

In half an hour she was clean again, and Silas having turned his back to see what he could do with the linen band, threw it down again, with the reflection that Eppie would be good without fastening for the rest of the morning. He turned round again, and was going to place her in her little chair near the loom, when she peeped out at him with black face and hands again, and said, 'Eppie in de toal-hole!'

George Eliot, *Silas Marner*

19. *The Bow of a Boat*

One object there is still, which I never pass without the renewed wonder of childhood, and that is the bow of a boat. Not a racing-wherry, a revenue cutter, or clipper-yacht, but the blunt head of a common bluff, undecked sea-boat, lying aside in its furrow of beach sand. The sum of navigation is in that. You may magnify it or decorate it as you will; you do not add to the wonder of it. Lengthen it into hatchet-like edge of iron, strengthen it with complex tracery of ribs of oak, carve it and gild it till a column of light moves beneath it on the sea, you have made no more of it than it was at first. That rude simplicity of bent plank, that can breast its way through the death that is in the deep sea, has in it the soul of shipping. Beyond this, we may have more work, more men, more money; we cannot have more miracle.

John Ruskin

20. *Steak and Coffee*

Then there is the beefsteak. They have it in Europe, but they don't know how to cook it. Neither will they cut it right. It comes on the table in a small, round, pewter platter. It lies in the centre of this platter, in a bordering bed of grease-soaked potatoes; it is the size, shape and thickness of a man's hand with the thumb and fingers cut off. It is a little overdone, is rather dry, it tastes pretty insipidly, it rouses no enthusiasm.

Imagine a poor exile contemplating that inert thing; and imagine an angel suddenly sweeping down out of a better land and setting before him a mighty porter-house steak an inch and a half thick, hot and sputtering from the griddle; dusted with fragrant pepper; enriched with little melting bits of butter of the most unimpeachable freshness and genuineness; the precious juices of the meat trickling out and joining the gravy ... and imagine that the angel also adds a great cup of American home-made coffee, with the cream afroth on top, some real butter, firm and yellow and fresh, some smoking hot biscuits ... could words describe the gratitude of this exile?

Mark Twain

21. *William the Silent*

He went through life bearing the load of a people's sorrows upon his shoulders with a smiling face. Their name was the last word upon his lips, save the simple affirmative with which the soldier who had been battling for the right all his lifetime commended his soul in dying 'to his great captain, Christ'. The people were grateful and affectionate, for they trusted the character of their 'Father William', and not all the clouds which calumny could collect ever dimmed to their eyes the radiance of that lofty mind to which they were accustomed, in their darkest calamities, to look for light. As long as he lived, he was the guiding-star of a whole nation, and when he died the little children cried in the streets.

J. L. Motley, *The Rise of the Dutch Republic*

22. *At the Auberge, Alexandria*

They were coming! The musicians struck out one long quivering arpeggio such as normally brings a tzigane melody to a close, and then, as the beautiful figure of Semira appeared among the palms, they swung softly and gravely into the waltz measure of 'The Blue Danube'. I was suddenly quite touched to see the shy way that Semira hesitated on the threshold of that crowded ballroom ... She hovered with a soft indecision which reminded me of the way a sailing boat hangs pouting when the painter is loosed, the jib shaken out – as if slowly meditating for a long moment before she turns, with an almost audible sigh, to take the wind upon her cheek. But in this moment of charming irresolution Amaril came up behind

145

her and took her arm. He himself looked, I thought, rather white and nervous despite the customary foppishness of his attire. Then he registered the waltz and stammered something to her with trembling lips, at the same time leading her down gravely among the tables to the edge of the floor where with a slow and perfectly turned movement they began to dance.

With the first full figure of the waltz the confidence poured into them both – one could almost see it happening. They calmed, became still as leaves, and Semira closed her eyes while Amaril recovered his usual gay, self-confident smile. And everywhere the soft clapping welled up around them from every corner of the ballroom.

Lawrence Durrell, *Clea*

23. *How to Look at a Church*

There's something much kinder about a house which has been lived in for generations than a brand-new one. Apart from the fact that ten to one an old house is better built than a new one, it's part of England, not a bright red pimple freshly arisen on its surface. An old house reflects the generations that have lived in it. Your mother's taste for frills and silk lamp-shades, your grandmother's passion for framed water-colours, your great-grandmother's needlework and heavy, well-made furniture. It may be a bit inconvenient and muddled, but it is human.

But of all the old houses of England, the oldest and the most interesting are the houses of God – the churches. Better still, they are open to the public, or they ought to be. Each generation has contributed to the adornment of an old church, and the result isn't a museum of showpieces, but a living thing, still in use. Old glass still diffuses the daylight on the latest hats as softly as it did on the wigs of the eighteenth century or the woollen hose of the people of the Middle Ages. Elizabethan silver is still used for the sacrament. And from the tower a bell, cast soon after the Wars of the Roses, lends its note to the peal that ripples over the meadows and threads its way under the drone of aeroplanes. The magniloquent epitaph and well-carved bust of some dead squire look down in breathing

146

marble from the walls, and the churchyard is a criss-cross of slanting, old stones. Here lies the England we are all beginning to wish we knew, as the roar of the machine gets louder and the suburbs creep from London to Land's End.

John Betjeman

24. *The Seven Ages of Man*

One of the earliest, and perhaps most disturbing, things a human child has to learn is that the course of human life follows the clock – it can be predicted in advance. When he is twenty he will be grown-up, when he is eighty he will be old, and before he is a hundred he will die. We take this for granted because we are familiar with it, just as we take for granted the fact that we have a characteristic size; we plan our lives in terms of it, just as we plan our houses, so that the few people who are more than 20 per cent taller or shorter than usual find them difficult to live in.

I suppose the main reason this fixed programme affects us emotionally is that it means we have a fixed life span. After a certain age our vigour and resistance to disease will begin to get less, and they will go on declining at a steady rate until some stress, which earlier in life we could have resisted, kills us. This is the process we call ageing. It is so statistically constant in man that insurance companies can guarantee us against early death, and we can roughly – though only very roughly – guess at the stage it has reached from a man's personal appearance.

Fixity of life-programme, if I can call it that, and fixed adult size are two things which are typical of warm-blooded animals. In cold-blooded animals there is much less fixity, especially in relation to growth. Many fish, for example, have no characteristic adult size; and some of them may possibly have no characteristic adult life-span. But in every warm-blooded animal there is a set life-programme which is adapted to the way in which that sort of animal lives. There is a set period of development before birth, a set period of pre-adulthood, then sexual maturity, and then, in the larger animals, the beginning of a senile decline. In the wild state this decline is cut very short compared with our old age; small mammals like mice never reach it at all, for their accidental death rate is so high that the rise in it which we call ageing never had time to show itself. But horses on stud farms and mice kept in the laboratory do show it: they age, in other words, roughly as we do, and their maximum life spans are fixed.

Alex Comfort

25. Hue and Eye

It is all very well to talk about matching colours, about making the vitriolic blue in this curtain material 'go' with the blue in that snippet of wallpaper, and so on and so on. But, just as we may wonder how fast the colour is in textiles, there arises the question of how fast are our colour perceptions. 'I came like water and like wind I go,' the poet wrote. There are conditions in which this forcibly applies to colour. 'One night,' Goethe writes, 'when I entered an inn, I saw in the dusky light a buxom maid with a bright white face and black hair. She wore a scarlet bodice. I looked at her closely, whereupon she moved away. Then I saw – imaged on the white wall which faced me – a black face surrounded by a halo, and the dress of the clearly outlined figure appeared to be coloured in a beautiful sea-green.'

Although perhaps less excitingly, Goethe's observation can be repeated with a red bicycle lamp: if you view it firmly for a few seconds and then look at the ceiling, you will get the impression that the lamp, seen with all its detail, has changed its colour to blue-green. The explanation of this effect is believed to be as follows. When the red torch is viewed for some time the light receptors in the eye particularly sensitive to red become fatigued. If we then follow Goethe and look at a white wall or ceiling, the flood of light stimulates all the colour receptors in the retina. But because the red-sensitive ones were fatigued they now respond less readily. So in the fatigued part of our retina we see all the rainbow components of white light without the red of the torchlight, that is blue-green. This follows from Newton's great discovery in which he demonstrated with a simple prism that white light can be split up into all colours of the rainbow.

R. A. Weale

The following book is comprised entirely of prose passages chosen by its compiler as being specially suitable for oral interpretation: *By Word of Mouth*, ed. Sansom, C., Methuen.

The following books are comprised of verse and prose chosen by their compilers as being specially suitable for oral interpretation: *The Lamda Anthology of Verse and Prose*, Volumes I–V. The London Academy of Music and Dramatic Art. Max Reinhardt.

POETRY

(a) '*The Discovery*' – J. C. Squire (see page 87)

The Discovery

There was an Indian, who had known no change,
Who strayed content along a sunlit beach
Gathering shells. He heard a sudden strange
Commingled noise; looked up; and gasped for speech.
For in the bay, where nothing was before,
Moved on the sea, by magic, huge canoes,
With bellying cloths on poles, and not one oar,
And fluttering coloured signs and clambering crews.
And he, in fear, this naked man alone,
His fallen hands forgetting all their shells,
His lips gone pale, knelt low behind a stone,
And stared, and saw, and did not understand,
Columbus' doom-burdened caravels
Slant to the shore, and all their seamen land.

(b) *Easier Verse*

		Number of lines	Source
Armstrong, M.	*Mrs Reece Laughs*	20	(15)*
Armstrong, M.	*Miss Thompson Visits the Bootmaker*	40	(15)
Blake, W.	*The Little Black Boy*	28	(16)
Blunden, E.	*The Poor Man's Pig*	14	(18)

* The number in brackets refers to the title of the book in which the poem is to be found under Sources, pp. 154–155.

L

		Number of lines	Source
Browning, R.	An Incident of the French Camp	40	(22)
Carroll, L.	Jabberwocky	28	(19)
Chalmers, P.	The Tortoiseshell Cat	20	(13)
Chesterman, H.	Christopher Wren	39	(14)
Chesterton, G. K.	The Donkey	16	(15)
Church, R.	Snobs	14	(15)
Clare, J.	The Vixen	14	(9)
Cowper, W.	Loss of the Royal George	36	(2)
Davies, W. H.	Leisure	14	(7)
De La Mare, W.	Four Brothers	16	(13)
,,	The Linnet	16	(4)
,,	Nod	20	(7)
,,	The Scarecrow	24	(20)
,,	Silver	14	(2)
,,	Tartary	32	(20)
Drinkwater, J.	Moonlit Apples	16	(18)
Dyment, C.	The Axe in the Wood	14	(15)
,,	The Swan	18	(3)
Eliot, T. S.	Macavity	42	(17)
,,	The Naming of Cats	31	(17)
,,	Skimbleshanks (1st stanza)	16	(17)
Flower, R. (trans.)	The Student and His White Cat	32	(15)
Frost, R.	The Road not Taken	20	(1)
Gibson, W.	The Ice Cart	38	(1)
Goldsmith, O.	The Village Schoolmaster	24	(2)
Holloway, J.	The Shell	21	(11)
Hughes, T.	The Horses	37	(11)
Keats, J.	Meg Merrilees	30	(7)
Kipling, R.	A Smuggler's Song	32	(2)
Marquis, D.	The Tom Cat	24	(26)
Masefield, J.	Cargoes	15	(15)
,,	Reynard the Fox (extracts)		(27)

		Number of lines	*Source*
Monro, H.	*Milk for the Cat*	36	(1)
"	*Overheard on a Saltmarsh*	20	(5)
Moore, T.	*Miriam's Song*	16	(7)
Nicholson, N.	*Wales*	24	(11)
Noyes, A.	*The Highwayman* (first six stanzas)		(12)
"	*Wizards*	21	(1)
Palmer, H.	*Prayer for Rain*	26	(1)
Rieu, E. V.	*A Dirge for a Bad Boy*	32	(13)
Sansom, C.	*The Donkey's Owner* (from 'The Witnesses')	18	(24)
Sassoon, P.	*Morning Express*	26	(18)
Sitwell, E.	*The King of China's Daughter*	16	(1)
Stephens, J.	*The Snare*	16	(1)
Stevenson, R. L.	*From a Railway Carriage*	36	(7)
Tessimond, A.	*Cats*	16	(21)
Thompson, F.	*To a Snowflake*	22	(3)
Turner, W. J.	*Romance*	28	(1)
Warner, R.	*Nile Fishermen*	20	(1)
Watson, W.	*Semmerwater*	38	
Wordsworth, W.	*Daffodils*	24	(3)
Young, A.	*Reflections on the River*	16	(11)

(c) *More difficult verse*

Arnold, M.	*Dover Beach*	36	(3)
Atthill, R.	*Columbus*	14	(1)
Auden, W. H.	*Musee des Beaux Arts*	21	(1)
The Bible.	*David's Lament* (*II Samuel*)	28	(6)
"	*Vanity of Vanities* (*Ecclesiastes*)	32	(6)
Blunden, E.	*Forefathers*	36	(3)
"	*The Pike*	30	(4)
Christ Church MS.	*Preparations*	30	(3)

		Number of lines	Source
Clare, J.	*Hares at Play*	14	(9)
,,	*Summer Evening*	14	(9)
Coleridge, S. T.	*Kubla Khan* (first 2 stanzas)	36	(16)
De La Mare, W.	*All That's Past*	24	(5)
,,	*The Listeners*	36	(19)
Flecker, J.	*The Old Ships*	31	(4)
,,	*To a Poet a Thousand Years Hence*	24	(5)
Graves, R.	*1805*	30	(3)
Groom, I. S.	*Jane, Queen of England*	16	(1)
Hardy, T.	*Afterwards*	20	(6)
Hogg, J.	*The Skylark*	24	(7)
Hopkins, G. M.	*Inversnaid*	16	(4)
Housman, A. E.	*Bredon Hill*	35	(3)
Johnson, S.	*Long Expected One and Twenty*	28	(3)
Keats, J.	*Ode on a Grecian Urn* (first 2 stanzas)	20	(3)
,,	*On First Looking into Chapman's Homer*	14	(2)
,,	*A Thing of Beauty is a Joy Forever*	24	(3)
,,	*When I have Fears*	14	(3)
Keys, S.	*William Wordsworth*	14	(3)
Lee, L.	*Milkmaid*	16	(1)
MacNeice, L.	*Morning Sun*	24	(25)
,,	*Prayer before Birth*	39	(10)
,,	*Prognosis*	36	(25)
Muir, E.	*Suburban Dream*	25	(1)
Nash, O.	*England Expects*	24	(23)
,,	*Very Like a Whale*	26	(23)
Nicholson, N.	*Rising Five*	25	(1)
Patmore, C.	*The Toys*	33	(16)

		Number of lines	*Source*
Pitter, R.	*The Tall Fruit Trees*	36	(1)
Pope, A.	*Hampton Court* (from *The Rape of the Lock*)	18	(3)
Pound, E.	*The River Merchant's Wife: a Letter*	29	(1)
Reed, H.	*Naming of Parts*	30	(10)
Ridler, A.	*For a Christening*	24	(1)
Roberts, M.	*'Already', said my host*	19	(1)
Sansom, C.	*The Rich Young Ruler* (from '*The Witnesses*')	33	(24)
Seraillier, I.	*The Squirrel*	36	(1)
Shelley, P. B.	*Ozymandias*	14	(15)
Shirley, J.	*Death the Leveller*	24	(15)
Sitwell, E.	*Still Falls the Rain*	33	(1)
Sitwell, O.	*On the Coast of Coromandel*	34	(3)
,,	*Winter the Huntsman*	20	(4)
Snaith, S.	*Parachute*	14	(15)
Spender, S.	*The Express*	27	(1)
,,	*The Landscape near an Aerodrome*	31	(4)
,,	*Pylons*	16	(3)
Stanley-Wrench, M.	*An Old Man's Hands*	22	(1)
Tennyson, A.	*Ulysses* (from 'There lies the Port')	27	(21)
Thomas, D.	*And Death Shall Have no Dominion*	27	(1)
Thomas, E.	*Adlestrop*	16	(4)
Treece, H.	*Bird's Skull*	22	(1)
Turner, W. J.	*Ecstasy*	25	(1)
Whitman, W.	*Miracles*	23	(14)
,,	*To a Locomotive in Winter*	25	(14)
,,	*Sparkles from the Wheel*	16	(14)

		Number of lines	Source
Wordsworth, W.	*The Prelude* (from 'And in the frosty season when the sun was set')	22	(6)
Willey, M.	*Tiger at the Zoo*	25	(1)
Yeats, W. B.	*The Cap and Bells*	36	(8)
,,	*The Wild Swans at Coole*	30	(8)
Young, G. W.	*The Cragsman*	36	(4)

Sources

1. *The School Book of Modern Verse* — Boas — Macmillan
2. *Verses Worth Remembering* — Maxwell — Macmillan
3. *A Galaxy of Poems Old and New* — Parker — Longmans
4. *Modern Poetry* — Parker — Longmans Green
5. *Georgian Poetry* — Reeves — Penguin
6. *The Poet's World* — Reeves — Heinemann
7. *Take Your Choice* — Stone — Harrap
8. *Selected Poetry: Yeats* — Jeffares — Macmillan
9. *Selected Poems: Clare* — Reeves — Heinemann
10. *The Penguin Book of Contemporary Verse* — Allott — Penguin
11. *Anthology of Modern Verse 1940–1960* — Jennings — Methuen
12. *Poems Old and New* — Cairncross — Macmillan
13. *A Poetry Speaking Anthology Book II* — Adams and Croasdell — Methuen
14. *A Poetry Speaking Anthology Book III* — Adams and Croasdell — Methuen
15. *Collected Poems Series Three* — ATCDE — Methuen
16. *Oxford Book of English Verse* — Quiller-Couch — Clarendon Press

17. *Old Possum's Book of Practical Cats*: T. S. Eliot		Faber & Faber
18. *Young Pegasus IV-V*	Simpson	Bell
19. *Orpheus II*	Reeves	Heinemann
20. *Sheldon Book of Verse I*	Smith and Wilkins	Oxford
21. *Sheldon Book of Verse IV*	,,	,,
22. *Narrative Art in Verse*	Clay	Murray
23. *Collected Verse*: Ogden Nash		Faber
24. *Poems 1951*		Penguin
25. *Collected Poems*: L. MacNiece		Faber
26. *Poems and Portraits*: Don Marquis		Doubleday
27. *Collected Poems*: John Masefield		Heinemann

The following books are comprised entirely of verse chosen by their compilers as being specially suitable for oral interpretation:

The Pattern of Poetry, the Poetry Society's Verse Speaking Anthology, ed. Seymour, W. and Smith, J.

A Poetry Speaking Anthology, Books II and III, ed. Adams, H. and Croasdell, A. Methuen.

The Poet Speaks, ed. Gullan, M. and Sansom, C. Methuen.

The following books are comprised of verse and prose chosen by their compilers as being specially suitable for oral interpretation:

The Lamda Anthology of Verse and Prose, Volumes I-V, The London Academy of Music and Dramatic Art, ed. Reinhardt, M.

1. The test is in two parts: Prose Reading and Conversation. You are asked to make 4 judgements for each part – 3 'details' and a General Impression. These judgements total 8 separate marks for each candidate.

2. The Rating Scale

(i) You will see that the Scale has 5 grades broken down into 11 marks (an 11-point scale, 0 – 10 inclusive).

$$9, 10$$
$$7, 8$$
$$4, 5, 6$$
$$2, 3$$
$$0, 1.$$

First choose the grade and then the actual rating marks within that grade; then put your chosen mark in the appropriate box against the 'detail' you are judging. (Award the marks for the 'details' during the course of the Prose Reading, those for the Conversation immediately after this item is concluded.)

(ii) When the Prose Reading is finished award a General Impression mark on the whole performance; similarly after the Conversation. Let each General Impression mark be a quite separate assessment (*not* an addition and average of the 'detail' marks).

(iii) The descriptions against each end of the Rating Scale (9, 10 – 1, 0) are a guide to help you in your judgement of the mark to be awarded. Do not be afraid to use the ends of the Scale. (Judges are inclined to hesitate to give extreme judgements.) Marks should be thought of as relative, not absolute, measurements.*

Look at your results after the Test and consider the possibility of rearrangement. (A mental ranking of the individuals in order of merit, beginning from the ends and working towards the middle, is of great assistance.) But if you feel you cannot put any cases into the top or bottom grades do not do violence to your sense of rightness. In the upshot reply on your own professional judgement.

3. It is important that there should be no collaboration between markers and that your judgements should be entirely your own.

4. Be careful about the effect of Halo, the unconscious tendency to infer that a candidate must be good in all qualities because he is good in one. Try not to be biased by the fact that in one aspect of speaking his performance is very good; be fair to each aspect.

5. Pronunciation

Note:

(i) that Pronunciation should not at all affect your judgement of (a) Voice or (b) Diction except in so far as the making of speech sounds may result in a form of voice-production or enunciation, respectively, poorer than that described in the Rating Scale against the marks 9, 10; (c) Interpretation or (d) Power of Verbal Expression except in so far as ease of comprehension is affected;

(ii) that the General Impression mark should, however, represent

---

* In the long run over a considerable number of candidates (at least 100) try to aim at a distribution giving numbers falling within limits in the following proportions for the five grades:

$$10\% - 20\% - 40\% - 20\% - 10\%$$

your *impression* and that you should not try to exclude Pronunciation.

RATING SCALE

1. Prose Reading

(a) Voice

9, 10: Strong, pleasant, well-pitched (subjecting the throat to no strain), flexible, free of tensions; breathing well-managed and unobtrusive; adequate volume.

7, 8:

6, 5, 4:

3, 2:

1, 0: Weak, thin, tremulous, tight, husky, harsh, hoarse, nasal, inflexible, breathy, breathing forced; pitch too high or too low; too loud, fading weak, inaudible.

(b) Diction

9, 10: Clear, correct, crisp; final consonants adequately defined; unobtrusive, unaffected.

7, 8:

6, 5, 4:

3, 2:

1, 0: Careless, slovenly, indistinct, slack, defective, over-precise; over-aspirated. Sounds omitted, substituted, added.

(c) Interpretation

9, 10: Delivery indicates a good understanding of the passage – skilful phrasing, fluent rhythm, expressive intonation, flexible use of pace and pause. Mood appreciated and communicated. Easy to listen to. Good stance and posture.

7, 8:

6, 5, 4:

3, 2:

1, 0: Delivery indicates poor understanding of the passage; phrases too long, too short; jerky or staccato rhythm; overdone intonation, flat, sing-song (stereotyped patterns of tune) or otherwise monotonous intonation. Pace too fast, too slow, or arhythmic. No appreciation of mood.

2. Conversation

  (a) Voice

      9, 10: As for Prose Reading.
      Successful maintenance in conversation of reasonable standard of voice.

      7, 8:

  6, 5, 4:

      3, 2:

      1, 0: As for Prose Reading.

  (b) Diction

      9, 10: As for Prose Reading.
      Successful maintenance in conversation of reasonable speech standards.

      7, 8:

  6, 5, 4:

      3, 2:

      1, 0: As for Prose Reading.

  (c) Power of Verbal Expression

      9, 10: Lucid, cogent. Well-ordered arrangement of ideas. Spontaneous and fluent command of language. Evidence of capacity to develop a theme. Subject-matter of good quality. Vocabulary suitable and of adequate range. Idiomatic use of language.

      7, 8:

  4, 5, 6:

      2, 3:

      0, 1: Finds it difficult to say anything; or is verbose. Ideas are muddled. Meaning unclear. Finds it difficult to develop a theme. Fails to keep to the point. Inadequate vocabulary. Uses slang inappropriately. Poor communication.

SPECIMEN MARK SHEET

Names of Candidates	PROSE READING						CONVERSATION			
	Voice	Diction	Interpretation	General Impression			Voice	Diction	Power of Verbal Expression	General Impression

B. FOR A TEST OF THREE OR FOUR ITEMS TAKEN FROM
THE FOLLOWING:
PROSE READING, CONVERSATION, POETRY SPEAKING,
AND THE GIVING OF A TALK

1. The test is in three (or four) parts. For each of the following (*or* –
for those items that have been selected) you are asked to make 4
judgements (3 'details' and a General Impression): Prose Reading,
Poetry Speaking, Conversation. For the giving of a Talk 5 judgements (4 'details' and a General Impression).

2. The Rating Scale

(i) You will see that the Scale has 5 grades broken down into
11 marks (an 11-point scale, 0 – 10 inclusive).

> 9, 10
> 7, 8
> 4, 5, 6
> 2, 3
> 0, 1.

First choose the grade and then the actual rating marks within
that grade; then put your chosen mark in the appropriate box
against the 'detail' you are judging. Award the marks for the 'details'
during the course of the speaking of each item, except for Conversation, the marks for which should be awarded immediately it is
concluded.

(ii) When the Prose Reading is finished award a General Impression mark on the whole performance; similarly for the other
items. Let each General Impression mark be a quite separate assessment (not an addition and average of the 'detail' marks).

(iii) The descriptions against each end of the Rating Scale
(9, 10 – 1, 0) are a guide to help you in your judgement of the mark
to be awarded. Do not be afraid to use the ends of the Scale. (Judges
are inclined to hesitate to give extreme judgements.) Marks should
be thought of as relative, not absolute, measurements.*

* In the long run over a considerable number of candidates (at least 100)
try to aim at a distribution giving numbers falling within limits in the following
proportions for the five grades:

$$10\% - 20\% - 40\% - 20\% - 10\%$$

Look at your results after the test and consider the possibility of rearrangement. (A mental ranking of the individuals in order of merit, beginning from the ends and working towards the middle, is of great assistance.) But if you feel you cannot put any cases into the top or bottom grades do not do violence to your sense of rightness. In the upshot rely on your own professional judgement.

3. It is important that there should be no collaboration between markers and that your judgements should be entirely your own.

4. Be careful about the effect of Halo, the unconscious tendency to infer that a candidate must be good in all qualities because he is good in one. Try not to be biased by the fact that in one aspect of speaking his performance is very good; be fair to each aspect.

5. Pronunciation

Note:

(i) that Pronunciation should not at all affect your judgement of (a) Voice or (b) Diction except in so far as the making of speech sounds may result in a form of voice-production or enunciation, respectively, poorer than that described in the Rating Scale against the marks 9, 10; (c) Interpretation or (d) Power of Verbal Expression except in so far as ease of comprehension is affected;

(ii) that Pronunciation should not at all affect your judgement of Organization and Content.

(iii) that the General Impression mark should, however, represent your *impression* and that you should not try to exclude Pronunciation.

RATING SCALE

1. Prose Reading
   (a) Voice
      9, 10: Strong, pleasant, well-pitched (subjecting the throat to no strain), flexible, free of tensions; breathing well-managed and unobtrusive; adequate volume.
      7, 8:
      6, 5, 4:
      3, 2:

1, 0: Weak, thin, tremulous, tight, husky, hoarse, harsh, nasal, inflexible, breathy, breathing forced; pitch too high or too low; too loud, fading weak, inaudible.

(b) Diction

9, 10: Clear, correct, crisp; final consonants adequately defined; unobtrusive, unaffected.

7, 8:

6, 5, 4:

3, 2:

1, 0: Careless, slovenly, indistinct, slack, defective, over-precise; over-aspirated. Sounds omitted, substituted, added.

(c) Interpretation

9, 10: Delivery indicates a good understanding of the passage; skilful phrasing, fluent rhythm, expressive intonation, flexible use of pace and pause.
Mood appreciated and communicated.
Easy to listen to.
Good stance and posture.

7, 8:

6, 5, 4:

3, 2:

1, 0: Delivery indicates a poor understanding of the passage; phrases too long, too short; jerky or staccato rhythm; overdone intonation, flat sing-song (stereotyped patterns of tune) or otherwise monotonous intonation. Pace too fast, too slow, or arhythmic.
No appreciation of mood.

2. Conversation

(a) Voice

9, 10: As for Prose Reading.
Successful maintenance in conversation of reasonable standard of voice.

7, 8:

6, 5, 4:

3, 2:

1, 0: As for Prose Reading.

(b) Diction

9, 10: As for Prose Reading.
Successful maintenance in conversation of reasonable speech standards.

7, 8:

6, 5, 4:

3, 2:

1, 0: As for Prose Reading.

(c) Power of Verbal Expression

9, 10: Lucid, cogent. Well-ordered arrangement of ideas. Spontaneous and fluent command of language. Evidence of capacity to develop a theme. Subject-matter of good quality. Vocabulary suitable and of adequate range. Idiomatic use of language.

7, 8:

4, 5, 6:

2, 3:

0, 1: Finds it difficult to say anything; or is verbose. Ideas are muddled. Meaning unclear. Finds it difficult to develop a theme. Fails to keep to the point. Inadequate vocabulary. Uses slang inappropriately. Poor communication.

3. Poetry Speaking

(a) Voice
As for Prose Reading.

(b) Diction
As for Prose Reading.

(c) Interpretation

9, 10: Meaning and mood appreciated and communicated sensitively and imaginatively. Skilful phrasing, fluent rhythm, expressive intonation, flexible use of pace and pause.
Easy to listen to. Good stance and posture.

7, 8:

6, 5, 4:

3, 2:

1, 0: No appreciation of meaning or mood. Failure of imagination. Failure to communicate. Poor technique: poor phrasing, overdone intonation (or flat, or sing-song or otherwise monotonous intonation), broken or staccato rhythm, pace too fast or too slow or unvaried. Speaker imprisoned in the metrical shape of the poem; or metrical shape ignored and lost.

Uninteresting.

4. Speech Making

(a) Voice

As for Prose Reading.

(b) Diction

As for Prose Reading.

(c) Organization and Content

9, 10: Subject adapted to speaker and audience. Central idea clear; significant subordinate ideas. Main points made clearly and effectively in a logically developing argument. A good introduction, body and conclusion. Material interesting, relevant, sufficient, of good quality.

7, 8:

6, 5, 4:

3, 2:

1, 0: Talk badly arranged. No logical development of argument. Main points do not stand out clearly. Ineffective introduction, conclusion. Material of poor quality, uninteresting, irrelevant, insufficient.

(d) Power of Verbal Expression

9, 10: Spontaneous and fluent command of language; clear, accurate, varied, vivid, appropriately idiomatic.

Standard of usage, range of vocabulary and conversational mode nicely adjusted to the speaking situation (the subject, the audience, the occasion). Subordinations used judiciously and effectively.

Good communication.

7, 8:

6, 5, 4:

3, 2:

SPECIMEN MARK SHEET

			Names	of	Candidates				
PROSE READING									
Voice									
Diction									
Interpretation									
General Impression									
POETRY SPEAKING									
Voice									
Diction									
Interpretation									
General Impression									
SPEECH MAKING									
Voice									
Diction									
Organization and Content									
Power of Verbal Expression									
General Impression									
CONVERSATION									
Voice									
Diction									
Power of Verbal Expression									
General Impression									

1, 0: Finds it difficult to say anything; or is verbose. Dull and uninteresting.

Language usage limited and inhibiting, inappropriate to the speaking situation. Poor use of subordinations. Meaning unclear. Inadequate vocabulary: slang used inappropriately. Poor communication.

APPENDIX 3 *Glossary of Speech Terms*

These are the meanings the writer intends to be attached to the words and phrases used in their individual contexts in this book. (The terms, Accent and Dialect, seem to need fuller treatment and are considered at the end of the glossary.) Where the meanings have been discussed in the text the page numbers are given. The numbers refer to the books from which the definitions have been taken; acknowledgement is made to their authors or compilers.

affective: having to do with the feeling (and emotional) aspect of experience.[2]

afferent: used of a nerve, or nerve-fibre, conducting a nerve-impulse inwards from sense organ to centre; synonymous with sensory.[2]

articulation: See pages 77–79

attention: See pages 48–49.

communication: the establishment of a social unit from individuals by the use of language.[1]

correlation: the tendency of two series of measurements to vary concomitantly, in consequence of which knowledge of one gives us a basis for drawing conclusions regarding the other according to the extent or degree of the correlation.[2]

criterion: In the context in which the terms *validity* (q.v.) and *criterion* are used in this book the criterion is a set of teacher's estimates of the ability in spoken English of their pupils. Thus a set of experimental test scores would be correlated with a set of criterion scores, supplied by teachers prepared to estimate the ability in spoken English of the pupils tested experimentally, to produce a correlation coefficient of validity.

diction: see *articulation*.

dispersion: equivalent to *scatter*, the spread or variability of a distribution of measurements, scores, etc., and measured by the mean variation or standard deviation or semi-interquartile range.[2]

distribution: the representation by a table, or graphically, of the frequency of occurrence of scores or measurements in the testing or measurement of a group of individuals with respect to a definite ability or character.[2]

enunciation: see *articulation*.

gestalt: form, pattern, structure or configuration; an integrated whole, not a mere summation of units or parts.[2]

intonation: the rise and fall in pitch (q.v.) of the voice in speech. Change in pitch is due to differing rates of vibration of the vocal cords.[4]

kinaesthetic: relating to the sense of perception of movement; the muscular sense.[3]

motivation: term employed generally for the phenomena involved in the operation of incentives or drives.[2]

normal curve: that distribution, represented by a bell-shaped curve, which satisfies certain mathematical conditions deducible from the theory of probability.[2]

perception: the process of becoming immediately aware of something; usually employed of sense perception, when the thing of which we become immediately aware is the object affecting a sense organ.[2]

pitch: the auditory property of a sound which enables a listener to place the sound on a scale going from low to high, without considering the acoustic (or physical) properties of the sound.[5]

pronunciation: (pages 81–82).

psychophysical judgements: judgements (or assessments) involving the relation between physical stimuli and sensory processes.[2]

ranking: placing a series of subjects in order, on the basis of some principle of arrangement.[2]

rating: the assigning of a score or quantitative mark to each individual of a series.

reliability: used technically in a statistical sense, of the consistency of a test with itself, i.e. the extent to which we can assume that it will yield the same result if repeated a second time.[2]

set: a temporary condition of an organism, facilitating a certain more or less specific type of activity or response, as in *mental set.*[2]

standard deviation: the square root of the mean of the squares of individual deviations from the mean, in a series; generally denoted by σ or S.D.[2]

subjective: pertaining to, or arising from, the individual himself.[2]

timbre: a qualitative aspect of a complex sound from the human voice, dependent on the number and relative intensity of the *harmonics* or *partials* present in the complex, and affording the means by which we can distinguish one human voice from another.[2]

validity: in statistics, of the extent to which a test measures what it is intended or purports to measure, which is determined by the correlation between its results and some other criterion of what it was devised to measure.[2]

vocal colour: see *timbre.*

voice: (pages 76–77).

voice-quality: (page 76).

ACCENT

'*Say now Shibboleth and he said Sibboleth; for he could not frame to pronounce it right.*'

'*Surely thou also art one of them, for thy speech betrayeth thee.*'

Accent is still the great divider – or, rather, the sign of division. As soon as a person speaks we start to classify. Unconsciously or consciously we pass a judgement: on his social status, place of origin, personality, character, the sort of mood he is in. Each one of us is a bundle of prejudice, experience and association, and this compound produces an attitude with which we confront our speaker. Similarity of accent may produce an immediate sympathy – we feel we share something of the same world. Difference of accent puts us on our guard. Accent may ease us into a new personal relationship, or it may hinder the development of such a relationship. Accent cuts deep. Attack a man's accent and you attack what is most precious to him – his home, his father and mother, his upbringing.

What is accent? Most people would agree that a major element is pronunciation. While this is, perhaps, the most obvious there are also intonation, vocal quality, enunciation or diction, rhythm and, perhaps, pace. Accent is both horizontal, that is to say, rooted in geographical areas, and vertical, i.e. it operates at class or social levels. It may also have personal elements. Intonation is mainly regional (although the higher up the social scale the less obvious, for example, the characteristic Oxfordshire speech-melody will be); it is also, of course, personal. Vocal quality or tone is mainly a class element in accent, although it is also, to a certain extent, regional. (Consider the nasality of Cockney or the harsh tone of certain areas of Lancashire.) It can also be a personal element. Pronunciation is mainly a regional element in accent although, up to a certain social level, the higher the social class the less obvious is the regional pronunciation. At this social level a man may be said to use an 'educated' Manchester (or London or Cornish) speech, in which intonation, voice-quality, diction and pronunciation reach a socially acceptable level and the pronunciation (and perhaps the intonation) suggests the region. Another regional element in accent may be a particular rhythm of speech compounded of a distinctive stressing and, probably, distinctive length of sounds and intonation pattern. Stress and length (if distinctive lengthening or shortening is present) will flavour the pronunciation. Pronunciation is a class and regional element in accent, but it is probably the least personal of the elements enumerated. The most personal is voice (or tone, or vocal quality or timbre). However much our accents may draw together in other respects we shall always be differentiated in this. Voice will carry to a listener a strong suggestion of the personal quality of the speaker, perhaps with undertones of social class.

While one or other of the elements mentioned may be more or less prominent in a person's speaking the total effect on the listener is one of *accent*. The listener is also an element in accent for he brings to his listening the sum total of his past. He is highly charged with voice and speech associations – associations of his own region, his own class, his own job. No two listeners will hear exactly alike for they will be 'set' to receive from a speaker different impressions of accent.

DIALECT*

Linguistically speaking, English is a language: the local types of speech of, say, Lancashire and Yorkshire are dialects. The Lancashire and Yorkshire types will now never become languages as much separated from the parent language as English is from German; but there is no inherent reason, linguistically, why, given the right sort of conditions, they could not develop. These conditions are social, political, economic, geographical – the exterior influences on language which play such a great part in shaping the development of the speech of any given speech-community. After all, the differences between a dialect and a language, the differences which separate one dialect from another, are simply differences of degree. Once a language has developed dialects – in other words once variations of vowel, diphthong and consonant are present, once divergences have occurred – then the conditions are present for infinite divergence. Thus have our modern languages developed from the original status of mere dialects.

The right sort of conditions for the development of dialect no longer exist in the greater part of the United Kingdom. Remoteness and lack of contact have given place to easy communication and crowded propinquity; rigid class barriers are slowly being undermined by the growth of educational opportunity. It is apparent that a large number of forms of modified Standard English are taking the place of the historical regional dialects.

---

* For this extended definition of *dialect* the writer is indebted to his friend and colleague, Dr K. Cameron, Professor of English Language in the University of Nottingham.

REFERENCES

1. CHERRY, C. *On Human Communication*. Wiley, New York, 1957.
2. DREVER, J. *A Dictionary of Psychology*. Penguin, London, 1958.
3. JUDSON, L. S. and WEAVER, A. T. *Voice Science*. Appleton-Century-Crofts, New York, 1942.
4. WARD, I. *The Phonetics of English*. Heffer, Cambridge, 1962.
5. LADEFOGED, P. *Elements of Acoustic Phonetics*. Oliver and Boyd, Edinburgh and London, 1962.

COMMUNICATION

Boulton, M., *Saying What We Mean*, Routledge and Kegan Paul, London, 1959.
Very easy reading. Deals very simply and clearly with the uses to which spoken language is normally put.

Hayakawa, S. I., *Language in Thought and Action*, Allen and Unwin, London, 1964.
A fuller treatment. Clearly and vigorously written.

Cherry, C., *On Human Communication*, Chapman and Hall, London, 1957.

Berlo, D., *The Process of Communication*, Holt, Rinehart and Winston, London, 1960.
Cherry and Berlo are both very readable but more difficult than Hayakawa. Cherry tends to stress the scientific aspect of human communication, Berlo the social and psychological. Together they form an excellent introduction to the study of human communication. Both have valuable reference lists.

University College, London (Communication Research Centre), *Studies in Communication*, Secker and Warburg, 1955.
A series of essays on various aspects of communication, each by an expert in the field.

LANGUAGE DEVELOPMENT IN CHILDREN

Lewis, M. M., *How Children Learn to Speak*, Harrap, London, 1957.
A popular and interesting introduction.

Lewis, M. M., *Infant Speech: A Study of the Beginnings of Language*, Routledge and Kegan Paul, London, 1954.
A scholarly account of painstaking research.
Lewis, M. M., *Language, Thought and Personality in Infancy and Childhood*, Harrap, London, 1963.
McCarthy, D., *Language Development in Children*, in *Manual of Child Psychology*, ed. Carmichael, L., Chapman and Hall, London, 1954.
Watts, A. F., *The Language and Mental Development of Children*, Harrap, London, 1946.

LANGUAGE AND SOCIETY

Jespersen, O., *Mankind, Nation and Individual from a Linguistic Point of View*, Allen and Unwin, London, 1946.
Lewis, M. M., *Language and Society*, Nelson, London, 1947.
Pear, T., *Personality, Appearance and Speech*, Allen and Unwin, London, 1957.
Pear, T., *English Social Differences*, Allen and Unwin, London, 1958.
Rossiter, A. P., *Our Living Language: An Englishman looks at his English*, Longmans Green, London, 1953.
A series of broadcast talks on accent and dialect in modern English society.
Bernstein, B., Some Sociological Determinants of Perception, *British Journal of Sociology*, 9, 1958, p. 159.
Bernstein, B., A Public Language: some sociological implications of a linguistic form, *British Journal of Sociology*, 10, 1959, p. 311.
Bernstein, B., Language and Social Class, *British Journal of Sociology*, 11, 1960, p. 271.
Bernstein, B., Aspects of Language and Learning in the Genesis of the Social Process. *Journal of Child Psychology and Psychiatry*, 1, 1961, p. 313.
Bernstein, B., *Social Class and Linguistic Development: A Theory of Social Learning*, in *Education, Economy and Society*, ed. Halsey, A. H., Floud, J., and Anderson, C. A., The Free Press of Glencoe, New York, 1961, p. 288.
Bernstein, B., Social Structure, Language and Learning, *Educational Research*, 3, 1961, p. 163.

Bernstein, B., Linguistic Codes, Hesitation Phenomena and Intelligence. *Language and Speech*, 5, 1962, p. 31.

Bernstein, B., Social Class, Linguistic Codes and Grammatical Elements. *Language and Speech*, 5, 1962, p. 221.

Bernstein, B., Social Class, Speech Systems and Psycho-Therapy. *British Journal of Sociology*, 15, 1964, p. 54.

All Bernstein's papers are of great value to teachers (who are advised to start with the article in *Educational Research*). They illuminate the relationship between social environment and language development in the individual and are likely to stimulate a revolutionary new approach to 'speech training'.

LINGUISTIC SCIENCE

Ward, I. C., *The Phonetics of English*, Heffer, Cambridge, 1962.
A simple introduction, excellent for beginners.

Jones, D., *The Phonetics of English*, Heffer, Cambridge, 1962.
A fuller exposition.

Ladefoged, P., *Elements of Acoustic Phonetics*, Oliver and Boyd, Edinburgh, 1962.
For teachers of speech an excellent introduction to acoustics, dealing with (amongst other things) sound waves, loudness and pitch, quality, resonance, hearing and the production of speech. There is a good glossary.

Jones, D., *An English Pronouncing Dictionary*, Dent, London, 1963.

Gimson, D., *An Introduction to the Pronunciation of English*, Arnold, London, 1962.

O.Connor, J. D. and Arnold, G. F., *The Intonation of Colloquial English*, Longmans, London, 1961.

Aikin, W. I., *The Voice: An Introduction to Practical Phonology*, Longmans Green, London, 1951.
Old-fashioned, but basically sound. Recommended as background reading.

Judson, L. and Weaver, A., *Voice Science*, Appleton-Century-Crofts, New York, 1942.
A comprehensive American text.

Fletcher, H., *Speech and Hearing in Communication*, Van Nostrand, Princeton, New Jersey, 1953.

Mittins, W. H., *A Grammar of Modern English*, Methuen, London, 1962.

A good elementary introduction to the new scientific approach to the grammar of English. Intended for use in schools.

Strang, B. M., *Modern English Structure*, Arnold, London, 1962.

A fuller (and more difficult) description of the grammar of modern English. Should be studied by every teacher of English.

Whatmough, J., *Language: A modern synthesis*, New American Library (Mentor Book series), New York, 1957.

SPEECH EDUCATION

Robinson, K. F., *Teaching Speech in the Secondary School*, Longmans Green, New York, 1954.

Weaver, A. T., Borchers G. L. and Smith, D. K., *The Teaching of Speech*, Prentice-Hall, Englewood Cliffs, New Jersey, 1959.

Two good American books on the teaching of speech in schools. Substantial in scope and size.

Baird, A. C., and Knower, F., *Essentials of General Speech*, McGraw-Hill, London, 1952.

Parrish, W., *Reading Aloud*, The Ronald Press Co., New York, 1953.

Hahn, E., Lomas, C. W., Hargis, D. E. and Vandraegen, D., *Basic Voice Training for Speech*, McGraw-Hill, London, 1957.

Three more good American books for teachers of speech.

Thompson, W. N., *Fundamentals of Communication*, McGraw-Hill, London, 1957.

A useful American text-book for teachers, the fundamentals being reading, writing, speaking and listening.

Burton, E. J., *Teaching English through Self Expression*, Evans Bros., London.

An excellent manual of lively and intelligent exercises in spoken English for all stages of the secondary school.

Gurrey, P., *Teaching the Mother Tongue in Secondary Schools*, Longmans, London, 1958.

Lewis, M. M., *The Teaching of English in Schools*, University of London Press, London, 1942.

These books contain good sections on Spoken English.

Thurburn, G., *Voice and Speech: an Introduction*, Nisbet, London, 1957.

Ministry of Education, *Pamphlet No. 26: Language*, H.M.S.O.

Bernstein, B., Bernstein's papers should be read for their implications concerning the teaching of spoken English. He raises alarming questions.

THE TESTING OF SPOKEN ENGLISH

Department of Education and Science, *The Examining of English Language*, H.M.S.O., 1964.

Burniston, C., *What is Spoken English? Can it be examined in General English?* The English Speaking Board, Liverpool, 1962.

Burniston, C., *Concord Through the Spoken Word*, The English Speaking Board, Liverpool, 1965.

Henry, E., *Spoken English Examined: Widening Horizons*, The English Speaking Board, Liverpool, 1964.

Hitchman, P. J., The Testing of Spoken English: A Review of Research, *Educational Research*, November, 1964.

Robinson, K. F., *Teaching Speech in the Secondary School*, Longmans Green, New York, 1954.

Weaver, A. T., Borchers, G. L. and Smith, D. K., *The Teaching of Speech*, Prentice-Hall, Englewood Cliffs, New Jersey, 1959.

Wise, A. *Reading and Talking in English*, Harrap London, 1964.

APPENDIX 5 *Specimen Regulations of the Regional Examinations Boards for the Certificate of Secondary Education*

North Regional Examinations Board: The oral examination will consist of three sections:

Section 1. Reading

This section is designed to test the candidate's ability to understand a given passage of prose, to show his understanding by the intelligence of his reading, and to show his ability to interest a listener by the quality, clarity and liveliness of his reading. He will be presented with a passage of modern prose of about 300 words in length, chosen for its interest and literary quality, and will be allowed five minutes in which to prepare himself for his reading. The examiner will be interested mainly in the intelligence and vivacity of the reading, rather than elocutionary expertise. (20 marks.)

Section 2. Conversation

This section is designed to test the ability of the candidate to hold an intelligent, informal conversation, to understand what is said to him and to organize his own ideas and to interest someone else in them. During the year he will decide upon a topic about which he wishes to talk, and will prepare such material as he needs for background. The subject of this topic will be forwarded with his entry for the examination and will be passed to the examiner. The candidate and the examiner will discuss the topic informally, the examiner assisting in a natural development of the discussion. (50 marks.)

Section 3. Comprehension

This section is designed to test the ability of the candidate to listen to the spoken word intelligently, to extract information from it and to apply that information. The class teacher will hand out a questionnaire consisting of not more than ten questions, with adequate space after each one for the answer. The questions are not to be seen until after the reading of the passage. In a preamble, the class teacher will tell them that the questions are designed to test their understanding of the scope and general content of the passage, not of items of small factual detail. This is primarily a test of understanding, rather than of memory. He will also tell them that preference will be given to answers written in coherent sentences, and that they may take notes, for which paper will be provided. Notes may not be taken in shorthand. The class teacher will read the introductory material provided by the Board for each oral examiner.

After this he will read, slowly and clearly, a passage lasting from seven to ten minutes, chosen for its liveliness and interest. The candidates will then answer the questions, for which they will be allowed 30 minutes. (30 marks.)

South-East Regional Examinations Board: Oral examination Assessment will be based on the school's estimate of the candidate's ability in Oral English together with the mark gained in an interview which will take the following form:

A. A passage to be read aloud by the candidate, who will first be given sufficient time to read the passage silently.

B. Spontaneous conversation, with an interviewer, arising from the passage and/or the candidate's interests and/or books read in course work. The interview will be as informal as possible to encourage the candidate to speak in his natural voice and as freely as possible; the use of memorized material should be discouraged.

No time limit is set for the interview except that it should be long enough to give the candidate full opportunity to show his ability.

The interviews will be conducted by practising teachers and will be recorded on tape to permit moderation.

Regional variations in accent and dialect will be accepted provided that they do not interfere with the ability to communicate. Subject matter, accuracy of expression, range of vocabulary and clarity and fluency of diction are the criteria for assessment both in the interview and by the school.

Standard forms will be provided for assessment of candidates' ability in Oral English.

For marking purposes the school's assessment and the interview will be of equal value.

The Oral Examination will be taken by all candidates, except those suffering from severe speech defects and other handicaps which affect speech. For exemption each handicapped candidate must have a Certificate signed by the Headmaster or Head-mistress.

South Western Examinations Board: Examination A. Oral Test
This is intended to test candidates' ability to communicate facts, ideas and opinions, and to speak and read effectively. The test is mainly one of communication. Local accents will be acceptable so long as they do not interfere with communication. The test will be taken in a group situation, each group consisting of not more than twelve candidates. It will be in three parts:

(i) Each candidate will present a prose or poetry book which he has studied and will read aloud a short passage chosen by the examiner.

(ii) He will then talk continuously to the group for two to four minutes on a subject chosen by himself, and will answer questions from the examiner and/or his fellow candidates. Candidates may use notes and relevant visual material.

(iii) Finally, he will discuss with the examiner topics which will enable him to present his own ideas and opinions. His folder of original work might well, initially, provide a basis for discussion, but other topics in which he has shown an interest should be explored. This discussion will probably best be conducted in an informal atmosphere around a table.

Examination B. Oral Test

Regional accents will be fully acceptable provided that they can clearly be understood by persons not familiar with them.

Candidates may choose to be examined in any two of the following:

(i) Reading aloud a passage of prose or poetry and discussing its content with the examiner. (Candidates will choose the book or set of poems, and the examiner will select the passage to be read.)

or Reading aloud and answering questions on a passage of prose or poetry set by the examiner. (Candidates will be allowed ten minutes for preparation.)

(ii) Giving a prepared talk and answering questions on the subject matter.

(iii) Discussing a topic selected by the examiner from the school course work.

(iv) Listening to a prepared talk or reading and then discussing it with the examiner.

(v) Discussing a prepared topic with a group of not more than six.

(vi) Explaining the significance of a graph or histogram.

(vii) Presenting dramatically a passage from a play or poem. The passage is to be chosen by the candidate or candidates.

(viii) Improvising in pairs. (Candidates will be allowed ten minutes for preparation.)

East Midland Regional Examination Board: Oral Examination (20 marks)

As a certificate in English should include the whole range of language, a test in Oral English is essential, reflecting the importance and relevance to life of the spoken word. The candidate should be able to communicate ideas, facts and feelings effectively by means of the spoken word. All candidates will be expected to take the oral test but schools will be asked to notify the Board of pupils with serious speech defects.

The examination will consist of three parts:

(1) The reading, after a brief study, of a passage of prose lasting approximately three minutes. The Board will provide several

passages so as to give the examining teacher ample choice. In the reading the following points will be taken into account:

(a) Intelligent phrasing and inflection, to convey the sense of the passage.

(b) Accurate pronunciation of words.

Local dialect will be acceptable but slovenly speech will be penalized. (5 marks.)

(2) An informal conversation around a subject chosen and introduced by the candidate. The subject could, for instance, arise from work undertaken in the literature folio, hobbies, careers, etc. During the discussion questions may be asked by the examiner with the aim of fostering the natural growth of conversation. He may, for instance, seek clarification of a point raised; encourage the candidate to draw on personal experience; require the candidate to justify his point of view on controversial issues. (10 marks.)

(3) The teacher will award marks on the basis of the candidate's skill in spoken English as revealed during the course. Drama, class discussion, class debates and lecturettes will provide opportunities for this assessment, which will be accompanied by a brief comment from the teacher. (5 marks.)

Index

INDEX OF NAMES